the
Very **English**
Travelmate

by
Jeremy Butterfield
and
Peter Terrell

LEXUS

Published 2007 by Lexus Ltd
60 Brook Street, Glasgow G40 2AB
Maps drawn by András Bereznay
Typeset by Elfreda Crehan
Illustrations by Elfreda Crehan
Series editor: Peter Terrell

© Lexus Ltd

All rights reserved. No part of this publication may be reproduced or stored in any form without permission from Lexus Ltd, except for the use of short sections in reviews.

www.lexusforlanguages.co.uk

British Library Cataloguing in Publication Data
A catalogue record for this book is available from the British Library.

ISBN 978-1-904737-13-1

Printed and bound in Malta by the Gutenberg Press

Your Very English Travelmate

gives you one single easy-to-use A to Z list of words and phrases to help you communicate in English – with the Brits.

Built into this list are:

- cultural references that are useful for understanding comments, comparisons and comedians
- place names that have special significance and associations for the Brits
- types of food and drink that are hard to figure out
- some characters from the media who have become stereotypes for the Brits
- older words and expressions, which are often used by the natives in a tongue-in-cheek sort of way
- a little bit of that mysterious phenomenon called rhyming slang

On pages 190 and 191 there are maps of English counties and of the south and southeast of England. It is in the southeast that the vast majority of the natives live and it is this part of the island that your Travelmate concentrates on.

Some headwords take the form of numbers. You will find these listed in alphabetical order as though they were words. So if you want to look up 99 or MI6 or 1066 (all full of meaning to the Brits), look for ninety-nine or m-i-six or ten-sixty-six.

Speaking English

Your Travelmate also helps you pronounce some of those deceptive and totally illogical English names which look like one thing and sound like another. So, if you happen to want to visit an aunt in Bicester [bister] or need to ask a native for directions to a dentist in Beauchamp [beetchum] Place or decide to look up an old boyfriend near Marylebone [marlee-bone] Station, just read the pronunciation guides in square brackets and you will communicate. You might even sound a little like a native yourself.

You will also find a mini guide to good old Cockney which *moit elp yer git yer ed arahnd some ov the sahnds and fings wot Londiners come aht wif. Roit?*

Symbols and labels

There are quite a few symbols and labels in your Very English Travelmate, all there to help you figure out exactly what sort of English word or expression it is that you are dealing with. Here is a descriptive list of these.

| COLLOQUIAL | This indicates colloquial English, English which would be out of place in formal contexts. |

 This indicates a particularly prominent aspect of English culture, flagged up with an iconic teapot. An awful lot of teapots could have been awarded to entries in this book, but giving too many would be silly. If you really want to understand the natives, you should pay special attention to the teapot awards.

| DATED | These items are old-fashioned English, a lot of them still in common use, often in an ironic way. Understanding these words can be crucial. |

☒ English drink

	English food
IDIOM	There are of course hundreds and hundreds of idioms which you will have to know in order to understand the Brits properly.
MODPHEN	This indicates a modern phenomenon, a speciality of our days.
"___"	This is a quote that has become an idiom, a common tool in the Brit's vocabulary kit.
RHYMING SLANG	This is a most mysterious type of very English word play; there's a note on it under letter R.
SLANG	This is just what it says it is.
TRUNCID	The Brits love using these truncated idioms, or idiom parts. Everyone knows the missing bit, so why bother saying it? Well, here's the full form given, just in case.
	There are some names with pronunciations so unlikely that you'll never be able to work them out.

the
Very **English**
Travelmate

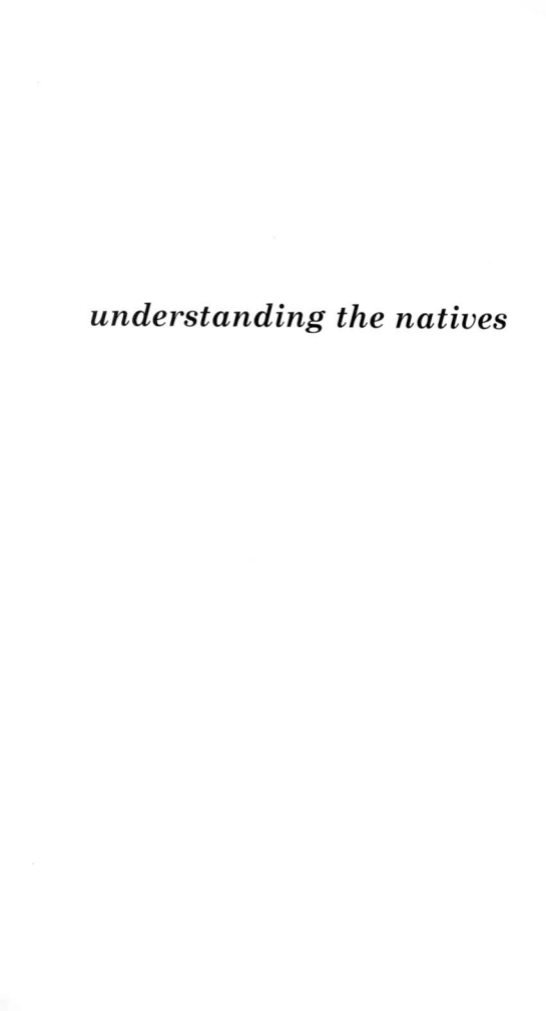

understanding the natives

A

Ab Fab a TV comedy series in which two not so young, very well-off women perpetuate adolescence while the young daughter of one frowns and goes for a conventional life

ABTA Association of British Travel Agents; looks after the interests of the travel consumer

ACA all calls answered, in the personal columns

Acacia Avenue mockingly symbolic of the ordinary English suburban street; some might say that the southeast is becoming wall-to-wall Acacia Avenues

actress → **as the actress said to the bishop** IDIOM used as a comment on a superficially innocent remark so as to give it a humorously sexual overtone; *that's the biggest one I've ever set eyes on – as the actress said to the bishop*

Adam and Eve RHYMING SLANG believe; *well would you flippin' Adam and Eve it!*

affluence → **I was not as under the affluence of incohol as thinkle peep** IDIOM oh well, maybe I had had a couple of drinks though

afterbule → **good afterbule constanoon** IDIOM a standard humorous reference to the manner of speech of the probably otherwise totally law-abiding citizen talking to the police officer who has just pulled him/her up for erratic driving

🍽 **After-Eight®** a small, square, chocolate mint, a favourite national small gift for dinner-party hostess, teacher, auntie etc

Aga® a traditional cooking range much loved by the upper middle-classes

ain't got no

> a colloquial and substandard version of *hasn't got any* or *haven't got any*:
> *I ain't got no money on me*

air miles MODPHEN Air miles are points which add up to give you free or discounted air travel. You can collect them in various ways: using a credit card, buying at supermarkets, taking up special offers etc.

air rage MODPHEN Because planes often can't fly fast enough to get obnoxious, self-obsessed people from A to B as quickly as they want, some of these people get drunk and fly into tantrums.

As they are grown-ups and not infants it takes the police and not mum to calm things down.

aitch → **to drop one's aitches** to pronounce, for example:

> *I hope you have heard him*
> as
> *oi 'ope you 'ave 'eard 'im*
>
> Dropping one's aitches is the sign of a downmarket accent. There is an odd but rarish countertendency to this, which involves artificially inserting aitches where none belong, in the erroneous assumption that this ensures correct and proper use of English: ***look Captain, what an enormous helephant!***
>
> Sometimes the letter aitch itself is pronounced haitch.

ALA all letters answered, in the personal columns

Albert Square the local square and centre of activity of all the characters in **EASTENDERS**

alcopop a bottled drink containing alcohol and a soft drink, packaged to appeal to the youth and female markets, sweet but deadly.

> **A-level** the exams, generally in three subjects, taken by students who have completed their statutory school education and wish to carry on studying. A-levels consist of two year-long modules, the first of which leads to a qualification in its own right. A-level results are used by universities and colleges to assess applicants.

Alf Garnett the foul-mouthed main character from the former BBC series Till Death Us Do Part, through whose mouth racist and jingoistic attitudes were satirized

Alice-in-Wonderland If you have an *Alice-in-Wonderland experience* or if an organization is described as having somewhat *Alice-in-Wonderland regulations*, then the idea is that of it being weird, running counter to the norm, having the logic of dreams.

-all

> Placed after a swearword, this gives that swearword the meanings of either:
> 1) no; *you've been sod-all help to your mum*;
> 2) nothing; *there's bugger-all to do round here in the evenings; there's damn-all you can do about it now*

Ally Pally COLLOQUIAL short for Alexandra Palace, a famous entertainment centre in north London housed in a palatial Victorian building

Ambridge the home of the ARCHERS

amused → **"we are not amused"** A saying attributed to Queen Victoria; *Deirdre, I see the gin bottle is suddenly three quarters empty; really, we are not amused.*

Angel of the North an enormous sculpture near Gateshead off the A1, a symbol of pride for the northeast of England

Angry Young Man a young man who is fiercely critical of accepted or prevailing social and political standards

"annus horribilis" Not an awful lot of Latin gets into popular speech these days. But the Queen made this one stick through using it in her speech in 1992. Now any bad year can be an annus horribilis.

another place the House of Lords; or, if said by someone in the House of Lords, the House of Commons

A1 a main road from London to Edinburgh

Apex Apex train and bus tickets are cheaper because you have to buy them well before the time you want to travel.

apple → **an apple a day** [TRUNCID] short for *an apple a day keeps the doctor away*

apples and pears [RHYMING SLANG] stairs

> **Archers, the** a radio programme that chronicles the lives of people in the imaginary English country town of Ambridge. The programme has been running nationally since 1951 and has, along with its bouncy theme tune, become a national institution.

Artful Dodger 1) Dickensian character, a youngster who earns his living as a pickpocket (in Oliver Twist); any ingenious, streetwise, dishonest kid; 2) [RHYMING SLANG] lodger; *helps with the mortage, your artful dodger, don't he now?*

Arthur Daly one of the two main characters in the BBC comedy series The Minder (late 70s through to the mid 90s), portrayed as an archetypal dubious businessman

> **Arthur, King** 1) a mythical king of old England, a symbol of honesty, courage and fairness; 2) a nickname for Arthur Scargill, a leader of the miners during their 1984-85 strike

ASCOT 15

ASBO antisocial behaviour order, an order made by a local council to somebody to stop them behaving in an antisocial way. ASBOs are highly controversial. In Britain's **YOB CULTURE** they can become prized acquisitions, trophies even, thus completely negating their purpose.

Ascot known as Royal Ascot, a week of horse racing at Ascot, near Windsor, and one of the highlights of the social calendar because members of the royal family always attend. It is famous for women competing with each other to wear the most eye-catching outfit, especially hats.

> **Ashes** a series of test matches in cricket between England and Australia. The ashes referred to are the cricket stumps burnt and kept at Lords cricket ground since an Australian victory in 1882.

Auntie a name for the BBC, not so commonly used these days, since the BBC doesn't behave like everyone's auntie any more

Avon® Lady, the a woman who sells cosmetics door to door

awful → "you are awful (but I like you)" a slightly camp catchphrase from the BBC's Dick Emery Show (1960s and 1970s)

awfully awfully COLLOQUIAL If someone is described as being *awfully awfully* this means they are very posh and speak with a very posh accent. They can also be described as **FRIGHTFULLY FRIGHTFULLY**.

A-Z® a well-known streetmap of London (or other cities)

B

B&B bed and breakfast in a private house, a cheaper option than hotels and a good chance to meet the natives in their own environment

B&Q® one of the nation's destinations for DIY materials and supplies

Babygro® a type of one-piece stretch-fabric garment for babies, which can accommodate them as they grow

Backs, the the grassy, pleasant area along the banks of the River Cam in Cambridge, stretching along the back of St John's, Trinity, King's and other colleges

BAFTA British Academy of Film and Television Arts, which presents awards that are the British equivalent of the Oscars

🍽 **bangers and mash** sausages and mashed potatoes, a traditional national dish, simple but filling

Bar → to be called to the Bar to qualify as a barrister

Barbars, the short for the Barbarians, a British-based rugby team which can include players taken from several home teams as well as from non-British teams

Barbour® a brand of waterproof country clothing very popular with COUNTY or wannabee county people and often associated with the GREEN WELLIE BRIGADE

Bard → **the Bard (of Avon)** COLLOQUIAL Shakespeare (no relation to the AVON LADY)

🍸 **barley wine** not wine at all but a very potent little beer

barnet RHYMING SLANG (shortened from the far less common Barnet Fair) hair; *just stopped off to have me barnet trimmed*

barrow boy COLLOQUIAL Traditionally referring to a man or boy selling goods from a barrow – a two-wheeled handcart – and a stock figure of EAST END life, nowadays it suggests the person described is coarse and pushy; *he may have loads of money but he's still a barrow boy deep down*

Barts short for St Bartholomew's, one of the best-known London teaching hospitals, founded in 1123

bean → **old bean** DATED COLLOQUIAL old chap, old pal; *one for the road, old bean?*

Beano® a very popular children's comic, which had its heyday in the fifties and sixties and features immortal characters such as DENNIS THE MENACE as MINNIE THE MINX

👂 **Beauchamp** [pronounced beetchum]

👂 **Beaulieu** [pronounced bewlee]

BEEF WELLINGTON 19

Becher's Brook [pronounced beechers] one of the enormous jumps that horse and rider have to clear in the **GRAND NATIONAL**

Beckingham Palace the residence of David and Victoria Beckham

Bedfordshire → **up the stairs to Bedfordshire** IDIOM to bed; one of the silly things that get said to children

Beds Bedfordshire

  bedsit a rented room in a house or flat which combines living and sleeping accommodation

bedsitter land Bedsitter land is an area where the majority of houses are split up into rented-out rooms, or bedsitters, usually inhabited by students or people not yet willing or able to get onto the **PROPERTY LADDER**.

bee's knees IDIOM 1) someone who thinks they're the bee's knees feels pleased with themselves; 2) if you say of something or someone that they're the bee's knees, you think they're great

Beeb, the the BBC

beef Wellington fillet steak wrapped in puff pastry and then cooked in the oven

Beefeater COLLOQUIAL a colourfully costumed ceremonial guard at the Tower of London, known officially as a Yeoman of the Guard

🍸 beer

> Don't go into an English pub and ask for *a beer*. The barman won't know what to serve you. So, unless you ask for a bottled brand, check out bitter, lager, mild, **GUINNESS**®. When you get to know your brands, it's normal to ask for your bitter etc by brand name or type; *a pint of John Brown and two pints of special, please*

beer → I'm only here for the beer
 IDIOM for the free drinks; for a good time;

not because I'm really interested in what is going on

Belgravia a smart part of London, with very expensive properties and lots of embassies

bell → to give someone a bell COLLOQUIAL to telephone someone

bendy bus COLLOQUIAL an articulated single-decker bus (as opposed to the old faithful double-decker)

beresk SLANG a deliberately silly contortion of *berserk*; *he'll go flipping beresk if he finds out*

Berkeley Square [pronounced barklee square]

Berks [pronounced barks] Berkshire

Berkshire [pronounced bark-sher]

best a shorthand for best bitter; *a pint of best, thanks Chris*

best of British! good luck!; often said in an ironic way

best → six of the best what teachers used to give pupils as punishment: six strokes of the cane

BHS British Home Stores. This is a chain which sells mainly clothing and household goods.

22   BICESTER

Bicester [pronounced bister]

bid A short synonym for *attempt* much loved by journalists; *tragedy mum in inferno escape bid (a mother attempts but sadly fails to escape from a burning building)*

Big Bang 1) the launch of full computerization of the London Stock Exchange, on October 27 1986; 2) the start of the universe (a theory)

Big Ben The natives like to quibble that it's not the tower but the clock's bell that is called Big Ben. But they call the tower (which is at one end of the Houses of Parliament) Big Ben anyway. It's chimes are resonant of Britishness.

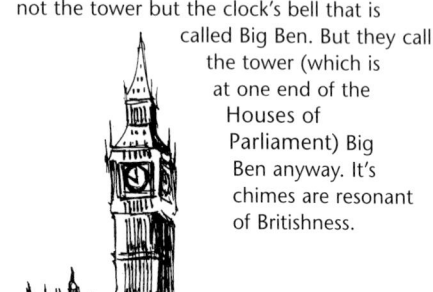

Big Brother 1) The term originates in George Orwell's novel Nineteen Eighty-Four and has become a synonym for a person or organization that exercises oppressive control over others; *don't get the idea that Personnel is trying to take on a big brother role, or anything like that*; 2) a programme in which a group of people staying together in one house are constantly monitored by television, so viewers can watch their actions and hear their conversations; a latter-day freak show.

big day IDIOM any important day but when used with a possessive pronoun, this will usually mean *wedding day*; *I don't want Dad spoiling my big day*

Big Issue MODPHEN a magazine created to highlight the situation of the homeless, who sell it on the street and thereby get a regular income of sorts

Biggles a boy's hero and pilot who was popular with children from the 1930s

bike: on your bike! IDIOM SLANG 1) go away; 2) general rejection as in: don't bother me with that, don't try that with me; *you want me to give you an alibi, on your bike!*

bike sheds → **behind the bike sheds** DATED where kids (previously) had their first cigarettes and/or their first sexual experiences

Bill, the COLLOQUIAL the police, also called *the old Bill*

Billingsgate the site of London's main fishmarket

bimbo COLLOQUIAL an attractive but dim woman

binge-drinking MODPHEN This is really just a modern name for a good old-fashioned booze-up. Binge-drinking is when people (usually young people) swallow huge quantities of alcohol in a short space of time to lose as many inhibitions as possible.

> **Birthday Honours** the honorary titles which are awarded every year on the occasion of the QUEEN'S BIRTHDAY (her official birthday)

bit of fluff DATED SLANG a dated phrase for an attractive but not very bright woman

bit of rough SLANG a sexual partner from a lower class than your own

bit of skirt SLANG any woman viewed sexually; *nice bit of skirt over there, eh Trev?*

bit on the side COLLOQUIAL someone you have sex with from time to time when you are already in a steady relationship; *let's get this straight, Julian, I'm not going to be your bit on the side!*

Y **bitter** the most popular type of traditional English beer, having a slightly bitter taste and a high hop content; *what's the bitter like round here?*

Black Country, the the once highly industrialized area west of Birmingham, named after the smoke from all the foundries that were sited there

black hole of Calcutta IDIOM a jokey way of referring to a place which is full to bursting with people, smelly and dirty; *on Friday nights, just before closing time, the King's Arms is like the black hole of Calcutta*

Y **black velvet** a cocktail consisting in equal measures of Guinness or any similar STOUT and champagne

Blackpool illuminations a lavish display of coloured lights hung from posts; Blackpool is a traditional seaside holiday town in the northwest of England; *at Christmas the Braithwaite's house is lit up like Blackpool illuminations*

Blackpool Tower Even people who've never been to Blackpool know of its tower, which is an English icon. Inspired by the Eiffel Tower, and at 520 ft about half its height, it dominates the town and can be seen miles away. Its top storey contains an opulent ballroom, scene of many radio broadcasts.

Blairforce One As soon as the press heard that Tony Blair was going to have his own personal jet, it became known as Blairforce One (his pal, the US president flies about in Air Force One).

🎧 **Blenheim** [pronounced blenm]

blighter DATED 1) a sympathetic way of referring to someone, generally male; *the poor little blighter got lost*; 2) an irritated way of referring to someone; *the ignorant old blighter belched right in my face*

Blighty DATED an old-fashioned name for Britain much used in WWI and WWII by British troops abroad but nowadays only used waggishly; *it's back to Blighty tomorrow*

Blighty one DATED a wound serious enough to have you shipped home to the UK, nowadays though you'll hear this only in old films; *poor old Roger copped a Blighty one*

blimey COLLOQUIAL a very mild and slightly dated exclamation of surprise or irritation; *blimey, is that the time?* ; *88 quid for that? blimey, that's not cheap, is it?*

bling COLLOQUIAL 1) flashy jewellery; 2) any kind of jewellery

block and tackle SLANG the male genitalia

Bloody Sunday a shorthand way of referring to 30 January 1972, when 14 unarmed Irish-Catholic civil rights protesters were shot dead by English troops

Bloomsbury an area of London around the British Museum famous for its bohemian intellectual life in the first part of the 20th century

🍽 **BLT** bacon, lettuce and tomato, a very English filling for sandwiches

blue An Oxford or Cambridge blue is someone who has represented his or her university in any sporting event; *Steve's a rowing blue*

blue rinse brigade COLLOQUIAL a dismissive name for women of a certain age who dye their hair

Blues, the a nickname for the Chelsea football team.

boat race 1) a famous annual rowing race contested on the Thames by 8-man crews from Oxford and Cambridge Universities; 2) a slang term for a beer-drinking race; 3) RHYMING SLANG face; *cor blimey, look at the boatrace on him, what's up with you then mate?*

bob a shilling in old money, which ceased to exist in 1972; never used in the plural; you will still here the word fossilized in expressions like; *that must have cost you a couple of bob!*

Bodleian (Library), the the main library of the University of Oxford

bog a slang word for the toilet

bogof buy one get one free

🍽️ **Bombay duck** not a duck at all but dried fish that is sometimes eaten with Indian food

Bond Street one of the smartest shopping streets in London, a byword for luxury and style and expensiveness; *she bought him a watch from a top Bond Street jeweller's*

bone → **on the (dog and) bone** RHYMING SLANG on the phone; *you still on the bone, woman!*

> 🫖 **Bonfire Night** November 5th, when the failed attempt by Guy Fawkes and other conspirators to blow up the Houses of Parliament in 1605 is commemorated by burning an effigy – a guy – on a bonfire and letting off fireworks. In days gone by kids on the street would ask you for a penny for the guy, ie some small change for them to buy fireworks with.

bonk SLANG very British word for sex or to have sex; *bonking Bishop caught with gaiters down*

Booker Prize the most talked about fiction prize in Britain and an annual media circus. There is a shortlist of six writers, whose chances of winning you can gamble on. The eventual winner can expect sales of their work to soar.

Boots® the most widespread and best known chain of chemists in Britain

booze cruise COLLOQUIAL a trip across the English channel to buy a carload or a vanload of booze

boozer 1) an informal word for a pub; 2) a person who drinks a lot

bottle SLANG courage; *after I clobbered him he didn't have the bottle to show his face round here again*

bottle it SLANG 1) same as BOTTLE OUT; *at the last minute he bottled it, bloody chicken*; 2) shut up; *oh, bottle it, for gawd's sake, you stupid moo*

bottle out SLANG not to have the courage to do something; *he was going to come rock climbing with me but then he bottled out*

bouncy castle MODPHEN a large inflatable model castle that children can play in and on, a favourite at kids' parties and fêtes

Bow Bells the bells of St Mary-le-Bow church in London's East End. Being born within earshot of these

bells is the traditional definition of being a true COCKNEY.

Boxing Day This is the day after Christmas, traditionally named after the custom of giving a Christmas box, or gift, to tradesmen such as milkmen, grocery delivery boys etc. Nowadays it's a day when people can go out shopping again after the pre-Christmas rush or just stay in and watch repeats on TV.

boy → who's a pretty boy then? IDIOM what old ladies traditionally say to budgerigars and what caption-writers might put under photographs of good-looking young men in newspapers

Boy's Own a paper specially for boys published up to 1967 which became a byword for a style and attitude; *Johnny Wilkinson's return to the England rugby team had a Boy's Own heroic quality about it*

Brahms and Liszt RHYMING SLANG pissed, drunk

brass monkey IDIOM If you hear the odd expression *a bit brass monkeys today mate, eh?* – the speaker is saying that the weather is very cold

brassic RHYMING SLANG (The full form is *boracic lint*) skint, broke; *sorry mate, can't help, I'm brassic meself until payday*

brew usually refers to a cup of tea, not beer; *fancy a brew, eh? I'll go and put the kettle on*

brigade

> You can call any group of people with something in common and who you don't think much of a *brigade*:
> *the blue rinse brigade,*
> *the jesus-sandal brigade*

Brighton bombing the explosion organized by the IRA during the 1984 Conservative party conference at the hotel housing key figures, including the then Prime Minister, Margaret Thatcher

Bristols RHYMING SLANG (from Bristol cities – which is not used) titties, breasts; *just the sort of bimbo with big Bristols that you would go for*

British Lions, the a rugby team made up of players chosen from all four home countries (England, Ireland, Scotland and Wales)

Brixton an ethnically mixed area in south London

Broadmoor a prison for the criminally insane

Broads, the an area of lakes interconnected by rivers in Norfolk and Suffolk and a popular holiday destination

broadsheet a newspaper such as the Guardian or the Telegraph, printed on a larger format, a more serious publication than a TABLOID

brogues sturdy, classic shoes whose uppers have a pattern of perforations

🔊 **Bromwich** [pronounced bromitch]

Brum a nickname for Birmingham

Brummie COLLOQUIAL 1) a person from Birmingham; 2) of Birmingham; *a real Brummie accent*

🍽 **bubble and squeak** left-over cabbage, potatoes and sometimes meat, fried in fat or oil. The dish is named after the sound the pot makes when cooking.

Bucks Buckinghamshire

Budget Day the day when the Chancellor of the Exchequer presents his budget to the House of Commons and hence to the nation. The contents of the budget are a closely guarded secret till then; *petrol's bound to be going up on Budget Day*

bugger-all SLANG 1) nothing at all; *there was bugger-all to eat*; 2) not any; *he gave us bugger-all encouragement with the idea*

bum's rush IDIOM if someone gets the bum's rush they are thrown out of a place, sacked or dumped; *only been in the job a fortnight and got the bum's rush already; Sally's given Damian the bum's rush*

BUPA [pronounced boopa] a well-known private healthcare scheme

Burberry a brand of clothing known for its distinctive check pattern. Once thought of as understated, classy and somewhat COUNTY, it has been hijacked by CHAVS and celebrities.

burk COLLOQUIAL an idiot

Burke's Peerage a list and family trees of the British aristocracy

butcher's RHYMING SLANG look (from butcher's hook). Not really perceived as rhyming slang any more though; *give us a butcher's at the paper, mate*

Butlins a holiday camp in some English seaside towns; organized activities for young and old

BYOB bring your own bottle, as written on invitations

C

Cambs Cambridgeshire

Camelot the castle and court of the mythical king of old England, Arthur

CAMRA Campaign for REAL ALE, an organization that promotes beer brewed by traditional methods

Canary Wharf the huge office complex and financial centre in London's DOCKLANDS symbolizing the regeneration of that area and containing London's three tallest buildings

Cantab A B.A. (Cantab) is a B.A. from Cambridge University.

Canterbury, the Archbishop of the highest ranking cleric in the Church of England, whose line of archbishops can be traced back to St Augustine in the year 597. The Archbishop of Canterbury anoints and crowns the British sovereign at the coronation ceremony.

Carnaby St a street in the WEST END of London famous in the SWINGING SIXTIES as the centre of the music and fashion industries

casting couch a couch on which movie or theatre directors supposedly seduce actors, the seduction being submitted to in return for being cast in a play or film; *it wasn't her talent that took her to the top, it was the casting couch*

cat's whiskers IDIOM someone who thinks they're the cat's whiskers feels very pleased with themselves, often because of the way they look; *in her Chanel suit she thought she was the cat's whiskers*

CBE Commander of the British Empire, an honour given to people who are judged to have made an important contribution to public wellbeing

CBeebies® a suite of BBC programmes,

website and learning materials aimed at young children

Chancellor of the Exchequer the cabinet minister responsible for government policy on all aspects of the economy

Charge of the Light Brigade a famously misguided yet heroic attack by a brigade of cavalry at the Battle of Balaclava during the Crimean War (1853-1856), in which the high loss of life shocked Victorian Britain. It inspired a poem by Lord Tennyson and the remark from a French general which has gone into history, "c'est magnifique, mais ce n'est pas la guerre". It is also used as a reference in modern English for a mad rush; *at 9.00 the shop doors opened to bargain-hunting shoppers – it was like the charge of the Light Brigade*

Charles Atlas a person with highly developed muscles

chattering classes, the that group of well-educated, thinking, socially and politically concerned folk for whom the world is not just a passing show to be watched without comment; the slightly negative ring to the phrase picks up on a perceived tendency to talk rather than act

chav COLLOQUIAL a sneering word for a working-class male of limited education who favours clothes, especially sports clothes, from specific designer brands; flashy jewellery or BLING is also a major chav accessory

chavette COLLOQUIAL the female version and helpmeet of the CHAV

chavvy COLLOQUIAL like a CHAV; *this makes me look dead chavvy, dunnit?*

Chazza COLLOQUIAL a press name for Prince Charles; *Chazza meets Macca at fund-raising dinner*

cheers COLLOQUIAL This word can be rather confusing if you're not used to British English. It is used:

> 1) when you take your first sip of a drink with a friend or colleague;
>
> 2) as an informal way of saying thank you to someone;
>
> 3) as an informal way of saying goodbye

Chelsea a fashionable part of London

Chelsea boots boots with elasticated sides

Chelsea Pensioner one of the small group of retired soldiers living in The Chelsea Hospital, a military retirement home designed by Wren, and completed in 1692. The Pensioners wear very distinctive red coats.

Chelsea tractor COLLOQUIAL A four-wheel drive vehicle, designed for bouncing across fields and rough tracks but actually used for taking the kids down the road to school and picking up the shopping.

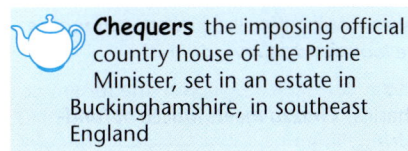

> **Chequers** the imposing official country house of the Prime Minister, set in an estate in Buckinghamshire, in southeast England

Cheshire cat Any reference to a Cheshire cat is a reference to a big wide grin.

Cheyne Walk [pronounced chaynee walk]

Chiantishire COLLOQUIAL a humorous name for a region of Northern Italy where the Brits have settled

chicken tikka masala

> People outside Britain may assume that the national dish is fish and chips, but according to polls the Brits' favourite meal is actually chicken tikka masala. Unknown in India, and possibly invented in Glasgow, this dish was created to cater to the British addiction to gravy.

Chiltern Hundreds a mysterious expression; if you read that an MP has applied for the Chiltern Hundreds, this simply means that the MP is going to resign

china RHYMING SLANG (the full form is *china plate*, which is not used much) mate, chum; *hello there me old china, how's it going?*

Chinese Fancy a Chinese? This refers to a Chinese meal.

Chinese bladder COLLOQUIAL a constant need to urinate; *three pints is not normally a problem for me, Chinese bladder tonight*

chinless wonder COLLOQUIAL a dismissive way of referring to a not very bright or determined member of the upper classes. It's possibly based on the idea that aristocratic inbreeding leads to a receding chin.

🦻 **Chiswick** [pronounced chizick]

🦻 **Cholmondley** [pronounced chumlee]

Christie's famous auction rooms

> 🫖 **Christmas cracker** an essential part of Christmas Day, these are cardboard tubes brightly decorated with glossy paper. Traditionally you and another diner pull at either end, the cracker makes a bang and releases feeble jokes, trinkets and paper hats, which the diners are then supposed to wear during the meal.

> 🫖 **Christmas stocking** a sock or sometimes a pillow-case used to put children's Christmas presents in, it is hung at the foot of the bed on Christmas Eve

chucking-out time When DRINKING-UP TIME is over, there then follows chucking-out time and you'll be asked to leave the pub.

Churchillian referring to or in the manner of Winston Churchill; *a very Churchillian turn of phrase*

CID non-uniformed police, the Criminal Investigation Department; *this is a CID job*

circular → **the North Circular, the South Circular** the old roads that circled London, frustratingly slow with their traffic lights and roundabouts, now superseded by the slick but congestion-prone and often frustratingly slow M25

City, the 1) a way of referring to London's financial institutions, the most important of which are located in the City of London; 2) the geographical area which was the original London and has its own Lord Mayor and corporation

city banker RHYMING SLANG wanker, stupid person; *my husband's a big city banker, you know, she said to the puzzled guests*

clap, the COLLOQUIAL gonorrhea

close your eyes and think of England IDIOM 1) a humorous phrase referring to people having sex as a duty rather than a pleasure; *he is stinking rich, so well, you know, close your eyes and think of England*; 2) also used in a broader sense of getting on with something which you would rather not do

club → **in the (pudding) club** COLLOQUIAL pregnant

club → **join the club, welcome to the club** COLLOQUIAL me too, so am I; we're all in the same situation

Co Durham County Durham

cobblers RHYMING SLANG (from cobbler's awls; the full form is not used any more) balls, nonsense, rubbish; *he's talking a load of cobblers; you've got a lot of money, ain't you mate? – cobblers (no, I bloody don't)*

cock → **me old cock** COLLOQUIAL a rather dated or joking way for a man to address a friend or to be friendly

Cockney 1) strictly speaking, a person born within the sound of Bow Bells in London, or more generally any London east ender with a marked accent; 2) the way of speaking that is typical of Cockneys; *as real as an American actor trying to speak Cockney*

> Some main features of Cockney (and the speech of ESSEX MAN and ESTUARY ENGLISH speakers) are
>
> *th* → *f* or *v*
> mouth becomes *mouf*
> three becomes *free*
> mother becomes *muvver*
>
> *ou* → *ar* or *ah*
> out becomes *art*
> Southend becomes *Sahfend*
>
> *i* → *oi*
> nice becomes *noice*
> time becomes *toim*

> h is dropped
> *hoop* becomes *oop*
> *how* becomes *ah*
>
> t is dropped
> *motor* becomes *mo'uh*
> *water* becomes *wa'uh*

Cockney sparra COLLOQUIAL an affectionate way of referring to a Cockney with lots of personality, *sparra* representing the Cockney pronunciation of sparrow; *Billy's a real Cockney sparra*

coco → **I should coco** COLLOQUIAL not likely, you must be joking, do you think I'm daft; *what? me let him know my PIN? I should coco!*

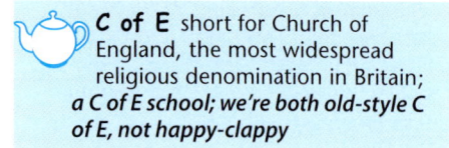

> **C of E** short for Church of England, the most widespread religious denomination in Britain; *a C of E school; we're both old-style C of E, not happy-clappy*

coffee-table book MODPHEN an imposing, glossy, illustrated book which is placed ostentatiously on a coffee table or similar surface and will, though unread, declare its owner a person of superior taste and advanced ideas

Colemanballs a section in the magazine PRIVATE EYE which specializes in publishing quotations of absurdly garbled, pretentious or meaningless English. The name, Colemanballs, comes from *balls* (rubbish) and *Coleman* a sports commentator, called David Coleman. So, for example, if I were to say; *if that shot had gone in it would have been a goal* – you would be quite justified in retorting *Colemanballs!*

Comet® a store specializing in discounted electrical and electronic goods

Comic Relief a charitable organization responsible for an annual British event, RED NOSE DAY, in which tens of thousands of ordinary people and celebrities willingly make exhibitions of themselves in order to raise money for charity

Common Entrance (Exam) the exams to qualify for entry into a PUBLIC SCHOOL, taken at the age of 11 or 13

Commons, the the House of Commons, the lower chamber of the British Parliament

comprehensive short for a *comprehensive school*, a secondary school which admits students of all ability levels from a given area

conkers an ancient children's game of skill, in which two combatants aim a conker

– a chestnut – threaded on a string at their opponent's conker and attempt to break it. There is an annual world tournament which raises money for charity.

constructive dismissal this happens when an employer changes a person's job so as to make that person unhappy doing the job to the extent that they quit, the employer thereby considering himself not liable to pay any form of compensation

🍽 **continental breakfast** a lightweight alternative to the ENGLISH BREAKFAST consisting of fare which is supposedly healthy, such as juice, croissants, rolls and coffee

Cool Britannia a NEW LABOUR replacement for RULE BRITANNIA, style in place of might

cor blimey a variation on GOR BLIMEY

CORGI The Confederation for the registration of gas installers; *before you get him to fix the central heating boiler make sure he's a CORGI*

corgi a type of short legged dog of which the Queen is particulary fond; *the royal corgis got off the train first*

corgi

> **Coronation Street** the longest running TV soap in Britain and still one of the most popular. It is set in the fictional suburb of Weatherfield, Manchester and deals with the lives of generally ordinary and unglamorous people.

Corrie a nickname for CORONATION STREET

Costa del Crime a TABLOID way of referring to the Spanish Costa del Sol, a favourite haunt of British criminals who have managed to escape the long arm of the law

Cotswolds an area of gently rolling hills in the southwest of England, full of picturesque villages and providing a relaxing country retreat for the rich, COUNTY people, and HRH the Prince of Wales

Countryside Alliance a campaigning and lobbying organization that champions rural interests, seen as opposed to the prissy, Labourite, townie mentality that can only see the countryside as a place to invest in a second home

county → **to be very county** a county person is rather upper-class, tends to be conservative in attitude, and possibly takes part in country sports, such as hunting and shooting

cove DATED an old-fashioned way of referring to a man, especially a dubious one; *he's a queer cove*

Covent Garden 1) the area east of St Martin's Lane and north of the Strand; well-known for centuries as a centre of entertainment and once the site of London's fruit and vegetable market, it is now full of fashionable shops, bars and restaurants; 2) the Royal Opera House, Britain's premier opera venue, in this area of London

cover go to CRICKET

cover point go to CRICKET

cowboy COLLOQUIAL a cowboy is a tradesman or service provider who provides an incompetent – and probably overpriced – service; *what cowboy put them pipes in! Christ! look at the leaks!*

Cowes Week This annual regatta, founded in 1826, is hailed as one of the most prestigious events in the world sailing calendar and is also famous for the entertainment that goes with the sailing. Cowes is in the Isle of Wight.

🍽 **Cox's** a traditional type of British apple

🍽 **cream teas** afternoon tea served with cakes, scones and cream and held to be quintessentially English

cricket see diagram page 50

cricket → that's not cricket IDIOM used to object to something that you think is not fair or not done according to the rules; *using inside information like that is not quite cricket*

50 CRICKET FIELD

the main fielding positions in cricket

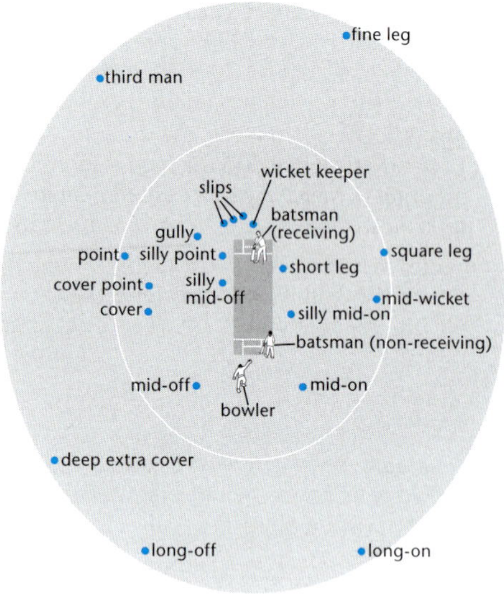

- fine leg
- third man
- slips
- wicket keeper
- batsman (receiving)
- gully
- point
- silly point
- square leg
- cover point
- silly mid-off
- short leg
- cover
- mid-wicket
- mid-off
- silly mid-on
- batsman (non-receiving)
- mid-off
- mid-on
- bowler
- deep extra cover
- long-off
- long-on

crikey DATED COLLOQUIAL expresses surprise; can be intensified as *crikey Moses*; **crikey Moses!, that's some hat she's got on!**

cripes DATED COLLOQUIAL a very dated exclamation of surprise, once used in boys' comics but now only ironic or journalistic

Cromwell Oliver Cromwell, the victor in England's Civil War and the man responsible for Britain's mercifully short experiment in republican government, from 1653 to 1658

croquet a game played on lawns, in which a heavyish ball is knocked along the ground by mallets through a set sequence of hoops

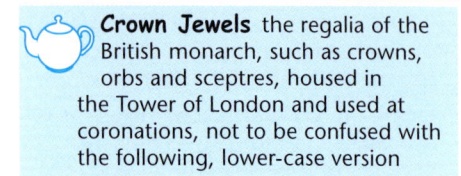

> **Crown Jewels** the regalia of the British monarch, such as crowns, orbs and sceptres, housed in the Tower of London and used at coronations, not to be confused with the following, lower-case version

crown jewels a man's most prized possessions, his genitals

> **Cruft's** a famous annual dog show

Cup, the the FA Cup

> **Cup Final** the big match of the English football league, also known as the FA Cup Final, played at WEMBLEY every year; the Cup is contested by all league teams from England and Wales. Scotland, however, has its own game.

cuppa COLLOQUIAL a cup of tea; *watch the news, have a cuppa and off to bed*

🍽 **custard** a traditional sweet sauce for pouring on puddings, traditionally made of egg yolks, milk, sugar and cornflour but normally now just out of a packet with custard powder

D

Dad's Army a hugely popular, nostalgic TV comedy series set in the days of WWII and featuring variously incompetent members of a group of Local Defence Volunteers, who were dubbed at the time *Dad's Army*

Dales, the Yorkshire the area of river valleys in West Yorkshire famous for beautiful scenery, traditional rural life and healthy, relaxing outdoor pursuits

Dame 1) a Dame of the Order of the British Empire, an honour given by the Queen; 2) a stock, older female character in pantomime who is almost always played by a man

Dan Dare an archetypal boys' hero and pioneer spaceman from THE EAGLE, a British comic of the 1950s

Dandy® a famous children's comic which, along with the BEANO, has created a string of well-known characters

darling

> Don't be surprised if a bus driver, barmaid, the cleaning lady or taxi driver etc calls you *darling*, they won't have fallen in love with you, far less

be making sexual advances, it's just an expression of the natural warmth and charm of the southern English.

Dartmoor one of the most notorious prisons in Britain, used to house long-term prisoners

Dartmouth a harbour town in Devon, site of the Britannia Royal Naval College, where naval officers are trained

day → **make my day** IDIOM give me the justification and chance to do something I would really like to do and you would not like me to do (from a famous scene in a Dirty Harry film)

day job → **don't give up the day job** IDIOM a humorous way of telling someone that their prized skill or talent is not really as good as they think it is; *it was a nice attempt at a novel, Justin, but don't give up the day job just yet*

dear a friendly and informal way for a person to address a customer in shops, restaurants etc; *can I help you, dear?*

Debenhams a national mid-market department store

Debrett an organization dedicated to recording the pedigree of the nobility and preserving good form in society, its publications include Debrett's Peerage, a list of all members of the aristocracy

deep extra cover go to CRICKET

Del Boy an archetypal lovable rogue from the hugely popular 1980s TV series Only Fools and Horses, his name is now used to refer to people who behave like him, setting up business schemes which invariably backfire or fail

Dennis the Menace a mischievous boy character, created in 1951, in the popular children's comic THE BEANO

Derby, the a major horse race, on the flat, held every year in June at Epsom

Desert Island Discs a long-established radio programme in which a well-known personality chooses eight pieces of music that he or she would like to take with them if they were to be abandoned on a desert island

Desmond RHYMING SLANG (from *Desmond Tutu*, the Archbishop, not Cockney slang though) a lower second class degree, a two-two; ***supposed to get a first, he finished up with a Desmond***

Desperate Dan a cowboy of superhuman strength and an iconic character from the children's comic THE DANDY

diamond geezer COLLOQUIAL a mainly London term expressing utmost approval for a man who is totally trustworthy, helpful and altogether a gem; *Jim's the bloke who'll help you, 'e's a diamond geezer, he is*

dicky bird RHYMING SLANG word. This is an instance of a piece of rhyming slang that has become a standard part of colloquial English; *that's Granny's present on the shelf, right, but keep quiet about it, not a dicky bird; honest, Mum, I won't say a dicky bird.* The expression has, in fact, become detached in meaning from its rhyming slang origins: *I didn't see anything, not a dicky bird*

🍽 **digestive** a sweetish, dry biscuit that goes well with cheese and coffee

Digibox® MODPHEN a device which converts digital TV signals so that digital programmes can be viewed on a non-digital set

dink A *dink* is a peron who has *double income no kids*; obviously they come in pairs; *Tricia and Toby are living the high life while still dinks*

DIRTY MAC BRIGADE 57

dinky A *dinky* is a DINK who is probably about to cease being a dink pretty soon, since they are someone with *double income no kids yet*; ***but they're still dinkies, they can afford holidays like that***

Dinky toy® a classic make of model car which every little English boy wanted in the 1950s. They can now fetch quite high prices as collectors' items.

🍽 **dinner**

> The word *dinner* can be a bit confusing. It can refer to the midday meal or the evening meal, depending on which part of England you come from, and what social class you belong to. In general, dinner is the more upmarket term for the evening meal (apart from school dinners, which are, of course, in the middle of the day, and Sunday dinner, which is at lunchtime).

dinner lady a woman who prepares and serves school dinners

Dirty Den a character from EASTENDERS notorious for double-dealing and womanizing

dirty mac brigade a slightly dated phrase for men with a furtive, unhealthy, masturbatory obsession with sex

dirty tricks brigade a name for any military or political group which specializes in undercover and devious activity, like destroying a person's reputation or getting the enemy to focus on the wrong target

disgusted of Tunbridge Wells COLLOQUIAL a name for the typically conservative or prudish person who writes letters to the newspapers objecting to changes to the status quo in any sphere, but especially in sexual mores or language; *when he starts on about binge drinking he turns into disgusted of Tunbridge Wells*

Dixon of Dock Green the very popular BBC series, starring Constable George Dixon, which ran from the 1950s to the 1970s and portrayed the police as an integral part of their local community. A famous catch phrase from the series was *evening, all*.

Dixons® a chain of shops selling economically priced electrical and electronic goods

DLR the Docklands Light Railway, an overground rail system serving DOCKLANDS. Trains run on an automated system and do not have train drivers. A Passenger Service Agent is present to man the train.

DONALD 59

do what? COLLOQUIAL expresses surprise, disbelief; *he cleared half a million in one afternoon – do what?*

Docklands the former port area of London, east of Tower Bridge, which has been regenerated over the last couple of decades

dog → **I have to see a man about a dog** COLLOQUIAL I am going to be absent for a while and I am not going to tell you why

dolly bird COLLOQUIAL a popular word in the 1960s and 1970s for an attractive and trendy girl; *he was famous then, he always had some dolly bird or other hanging on his arm*

Dolly the Sheep MODPHEN the first (living) animal to be produced by cloning, she won a special place in the British public's heart

Dome, the short for the MILLENNIUM DOME

domestic COLLOQUIAL In police jargon a domestic is a dispute or disturbance which occurs in a home and between members of a family.

Donald RHYMING SLANG COLLOQUIAL short for Donald Duck, meaning *luck*; *just my Donald, there goes the last train now!*

Donald Duck [RHYMING SLANG] luck

don't do anything I wouldn't do [IDIOM] Probably said with a wink and in an irritatingly jocular tone of voice, this is really an invitation to do whatever you feel like doing.

don't mind if I do [COLLOQUIAL] just a way of saying *yes, please*; ***more tea, Arthur? – don't mind if I do***

double first the best university degree you can get at the BA or BSc level with a first-class pass in two subjects

double-glazing salesman the stereotype of the high-pressure salesman, not seen as positive

double negative

> Double negatives are strictly speaking not allowed in English, since two negatives make a positive and the speaker therefore ends up saying the opposite of what he/she means:
> ***I don't have got no time for that***

double top a score of double 20 in darts

double whammy [IDIOM] a double whammy, while generally a combination of two bad things; ***losing his wife and father in the same month was a real double whammy*** – it is also occasionally used to refer to a simultaneous combination of two good things

down The word has a number of uses which have nothing to do with being lower.

> **down at Angie's** at Angie's place
>
> **down the pub** at the pub; *he's dahna pub in-ee*
>
> **down the road** further along the road
>
> **it's down to you** can mean exactly the same as *it's up to you*, ie it's your decision, your choice, you are the one who is going to make it happen; *it's down to us whether we succeed or not*
>
> **it's down to you** can also have the sense of *it's caused by you, it's your fault*; *what's all this glass on the floor? is that down to you?*

> **Downing Street** used as a name for the government, although only the Prime Minister and the Chancellor of the Exchequer live there; *Downing Street will probably play down the significance of this new development*

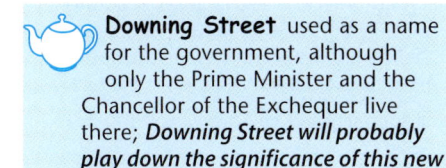

draught beer that is drawn or pulled from a barrel and through a tap as opposed to beer that comes from a bottle or can

dreaming spires, the the reference is the city of Oxford

drinking-up time [MODPHEN] the period of grace between the official closing time of a pub and the time when they throw you out, which varies in duration according to the location and social status of the drinking establishment, but is usually about ten minutes

drinky-poo [COLLOQUIAL] a little drink; *fancy another little drinky-poo before heading home?*

drop deadline [COLLOQUIAL] the absolute deadline, beyond which there is no hope of life for those that fail to make it

Drury Lane a part of London famous for its theatres

Dr Who the central character in a long-running BBC science-fiction series which has been cult for many years. Among his many powers is time travel.

DTI Department of Trade and Industry

duck when a batsman in cricket scores no runs he is said to have *scored a duck*; *Cooper came in and was soon out for a duck*

duck, ducks [COLLOQUIAL] an informal, rather old-fashioned way for a woman to address a customer in a shop, restaurant etc

duckie COLLOQUIAL 1) a friendly, rather old-fashioned way for a woman to address a customer; 2) an affected way for a man to address another man, especially if he is gay

Duke of Edinburgh's (Award) MODPHEN a scheme which encourages boys and girls over the age of 14 to develop personally and socially through a mix of community involvement and physical activities; *Nicholas did his Duke of Edinburgh's last year and had to spend two nights sleeping out in the open*

🎧 **Dulwich** [pronounced dullitch]

Dumb Britain a PRIVATE EYE column which focuses on the often stunning lack of general knowledge of the modern Brit, typically as vaunted on TV quiz shows

Dunkirk spirit IDIOM When people overcome a potentially disastrous situation by helping one another to their utmost they're displaying Dunkirk spirit, named after the retreat from Dunkirk in WWII; *two days to the formal opening and everything's going wrong, but don't panic, what we need here is a bit of the old Dunkirk spirit*

dunnit? COLLOQUIAL doesn't it?

Durex® a condom

Dutch → **my old Dutch** SLANG a Cockney expression for *my wife*

Dyson® a brand of bagless vacuum cleaner with a high design concept

E

Eagle, the a hugely popular boys' comic, whose heyday was in the 1950s

East End a once largely working-class area of London, to the east of the CITY and including industrial and dock areas. It is famous for down-to-earth humour, Cockney RHYMING SLANG, JACK THE RIPPER, and unusual food, such as JELLIED EELS, cockles and whelks.

> **EastEnders** One of the most popular series on British TV, set in the East End of London, but of diminishing interest the further north in Britain you live

easy-peasy COLLOQUIAL very easy, mainly children's language

ecky thump a stereotypical exclamation taken to be typical of Lancashire or

Yorkshire people; *ecky thump, lass, tha's fair puttin' ont' beef* (good grief, girl, you haven't half put on a bit of weight)

ecky thump vowels These are the broad vowels of Lancashire and Yorkshire men and women, which contrast with the either bland or rough sounds uttered further south.

Edgbaston a famous cricket ground in Birmingham

eeny meeny miney mo a choosing rhyme used to decide from among a group of people who will do or receive something, or to decide which of a group of objects is to be chosen; nowadays likely to land you in a pile of trouble because of the formerly included, and now unacceptable, use of the word *nigger*; the second line has been replaced by *catch a tigger by the toe* – a tigger being a tiger. The rhyme continues: *if he hollers let him go, eeny meeny miney mo*

elementary, my dear Watson IDIOM it might seem difficult to you, but it's pretty obvious and clear-cut to me. The line, now used for humorous effect, originates from the crime-solving gentleman and amateur detective, SHERLOCK HOLMES; *how on earth did you find that out? – elementary, my dear Watson, I googled it*

Elephant and Castle 1) RHYMING SLANG arsehole; *he got a kick right up the Elephant and Castle*; 2) a district in London

elephants RHYMING SLANG (the full form is *elephant's trunk*) drunk; *he staggered home elephants*

eleven-plus Passing this exam, taken at around the age of 11, as its name suggests, used to be obligatory for pupils wishing to enter GRAMMAR SCHOOL. Nowadays it forms one part of the criteria which grammar and independent schools use to assess applicants; *Donald says that a lot of university applicants these days are not capable of old-style eleven-plus maths*

elevenses Who has time for this nowadays? A snack that mum would have around 11.00am to tide her over between breakfast and lunch.

Ena Sharples one of the original characters in CORONATION STREET who was known for her outspokenness and no-nonsense approach to life

end of! SLANG short for *end of story*, this is an abrupt and sometimes aggressive way of indicating that you are dead serious about what you are saying and don't want to discuss the matter any more; *look mate, I'm not paying for it, end of!*

"England expects" Said by Admiral Lord Nelson before the battle of Trafalgar (in full: England expects that every man shall do his duty). Can now be said by someone about to bravely do his unpleasant duty; *giant spider in the bathroom eh? ah well, England expects*

English breakfast the traditional cooked breakfast, consisting of eggs and bacon and, optionally, sausages, black pudding and baked beans

Equity the actors' union; *we couldn't afford to pay Equity rates so we played the main parts ourselves*

Esq. short for Esquire, this is getting quite rare these days and is mainly used in addressing formal letters, as from a solicitor or an undertaker. It is used after a man's name, instead of putting Mr. in front; *Brian Warriner, Esq.*

Essex facelift SLANG a woman's hairstyle with the hair pulled very tightly back from the forehead

Essex girl COLLOQUIAL a dismissive name for a type of unsophisticated, loud and flashy girl typically seen to come from Essex

Essex man COLLOQUIAL a dismissive name for a type of unsophisticated, loud and flashy man typically seen to come from Essex

estuary English

> a much discussed variety of English named after the Thames estuary and spoken across much of London and the eastern counties, such as Essex. Key features include pronouncing the letter l as a w, and t gutturally:
> *awri'h, ma'hie?* (all right matey?)

e-tailing MODPHEN retailing on the Internet

Eton England's most prestigious public school, where many former Prime Ministers have been educated

Etonian an Etonian is someone who went to Eton

Europe This starts at Calais, the traditional view being that Britain is not actually part of Europe.

Eve's pudding stewed apples covered with sponge

Excalibur the sword of KING ARTHUR. It had magical properties and only the rightful king was able to pull it from the stone into which it had been thrust. On Arthur's death the sword was taken back into the other world.

Express®, the a middle-brow, somewhat conservative newspaper

🔊 **Eyot** [pronounced like the number 8]

F

FA the Football Association, the body responsible for setting the rules for the game in England and for running the FA cup

Fab Four, the COLLOQUIAL the Beatles

Fagin a character in Dickens' Oliver Twist who ran a gang of child thieves, he is a symbol of evil and miserliness and the exploitation of the young

fair do's IDIOM used to show that you grudgingly accept the truth of something said; *he's married someone half his age, but, fair do's, he was on his own for a long time*

Famous Five a group of four child detectives and their dog from the classic children's stories by Enid Blyton, written far back in the 1940s

fancy → don't fancy yours IDIOM a phrase used when looking for sexual partners to show that you don't think much of the potential conquest the person you're with is going to be lumbered with when you have made your own choice

farmers' market MODPHEN where you can buy produce (cheese, meat, honey etc) that has come straight from the producer and not via a supermarket

Farnborough an annual aircraft display, held at the airfield in the town of Farnborough

fat cat COLLOQUIAL one of the absurdly highly paid, usually a director

father → a bit of how's your father SLANG (actual pronunciation: a bi'uh ahz yer fahver) some sexual activity, the extent of which is vague; *somebody's been having a bit of how's your father, going by the colour of somebody's cheeks*

Fawlty Towers Once the title of a TV comedy series, this has become a synonym for any hotel where strange things happen and where the staff (especially management) are more than slightly odd; *our weekend break hotel was pure Fawlty Towers*

Fens, the a flat, marshy part of eastern England in the counties of Lincolnshire, Cambridgeshire and Norfolk, famous for its canals

Fergie 1) the Duchess of York; 2) Alex Ferguson, the manager of Manchester United football team

FHB family hold back; *there's not a lot of chocolate cake, kids, so, when the guests arrive, you know, FHB*

Financial Times®, the a serious newspaper which focuses on business and finance and which is, famously, printed on pinkish paper

finders keepers IDIOM a phrase loved by children but also used by adults to show you're going to keep something that you've found and the original owner will have to put up with having lost it; *I found it so finders keepers; you know what they say, finders keepers, losers weepers*

fine leg go to CRICKET

first a first-class honours degree; *everyone thought Brian would get a first*

fish and chips the fabled British dish of fish covered in batter (or sometimes breadcrumbs), served with fried potato chips and often liberally sprinkled with salt and vinegar, eaten, if you're on the go, out of a paper wrapping (or maybe a polystyrene box)

Fitzrovia an area of London to the west of Tottenham Court Road and north of Oxford Street

flash Harry over-smartly dressed, a little spivvy, not completely trustworthy, liable to take you for a ride

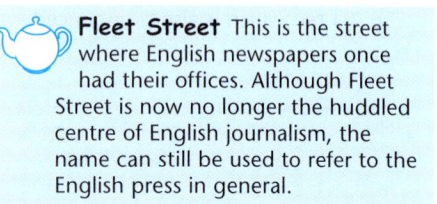

Fleet Street This is the street where English newspapers once had their offices. Although Fleet Street is now no longer the huddled centre of English journalism, the name can still be used to refer to the English press in general.

Florence Nightingale an Englishwoman who gained great national affection as a result of her toils working as a nurse during the Crimean war; her name has become a synonym for a caring but fairly strict and no-nonsense nurse; *you'll be all right now, son, here comes Florence Nightingale with the sticky plasters*

fly cemetry a biscuit which contains a lot of currants

Flying Squad, the a section of the police force that responds rapidly to a criminal activity

FO Foreign Office

footie COLLOQUIAL Footie is football. Not to be confused with FOOTSIE.

footsie 1) touching feet or legs with someone (of the opposite sex) under the table; *Billy hadn't realized that Greg was playing footsie with Caroline all through the dessert course.* Not to be confused with 2) FTSE, which is also pronounced *footsie*.

Fort Knox → **it's like Fort Knox** IDIOM the security is very tight (Fort Knox being the place where the US keeps its gold reserves); *you seen his garden shed? it's like bloody Fort Knox*

Fortnum and Mason® a very traditional and exclusive department store in Piccadilly, London, favoured by the upper classes and royalty and specializing in foodstuffs

Foyles® Any book-buying Londoner asked to name a bookshop is likely to put Foyles near the top of the list. Founded over a hundred years ago and still in private hands, Foyles remains a very distinctive brand.

free house a pub not owned by a particular brewery and hence free to sell whatever brands of beer it chooses (no free drinks)

French → a French SLANG a French is a blow job, oral sex

French → excuse my French COLLOQUIAL said as a kind of apology by a person who has just used strong language; *that Ernie is a dirty little sodding bugger, if you'll excuse my French*

French kiss a kiss when tongues touch

fridge-freezer RHYMING SLANG a GEEZER, a bloke; *that's the bleeding fridge-freezer what nicked me motor!*

frightfully frightfully COLLOQUIAL If a person is *frightfully frightfully* that person will speak with a super posh accent.

fry-up food cooked in the frying pan, typically sausages, bacon, potatoes, eggs, onions, maybe fried bread too

FT the FINANCIAL TIMES newspaper

FTSE the Financial Times Stock Exchange, the gauge of the London Stock Market.

FTSE100 index the Financial Times Stock Exchange 100 index, [pronounced *footsie*] a list published by the Financial Times of the share values of the largest 100 companies listed on the London Stock Exchange and used as a guide to how the British economy is performing

fuck-all SLANG Not a very refined word for 1) nothing; *you've done fuck-all all morning, you lazy sod*; 2) no … at all; *that's fuck-all use to me*

🍽 **full English** the same as an ENGLISH BREAKFAST

fun run MODPHEN a long-distance run (say 2-10 kilometres), the object being to offer a sports event for those who are not normally sporty and sometimes also to raise money

f-word, the

> a standard and non-offensive way of referring to *fuck* without actually having to use it

G

🍸 **G and T** gin and tonic

gaffer COLLOQUIAL 1) the boss; 2) an old man

Galahad A Galahad, or a Sir Galahad, is, in theory, a man who acts with perfect honesty, decency and moral integrity;

there he is, my Sir Galahad, the man who rescued me from a hopeless fate. The original Galahad was one of **KING ARTHUR**'s knights.

Gang of Four COLLOQUIAL One of the first new groupings to be seen in British politics for a long time appeared in 1981 and attracted the Chinese-style nickname of the Gang of Four. The four were Shirley Williams, David Owen, William Rodgers and Roy Jenkins. Their Social Democrat Party ceased to exist in the 90s.

gap year MODPHEN To make a break between school and university kids tend to take a gap year. The gap is usually filled with travel, odd jobs and experience-gathering.

garden gnome a decorative little creature, once held typical of suburban tackiness; you don't see many of them these days

Garden of England a reference to the county of Kent (whose future as such a garden must be dubious given the increasing water shortages)

gate

> It all started with Watergate in the Nixon era in the States. Nowadays

> *gate* has become a suffix that can be attached to any name to denote a situation that is complex, scandalous, fodder for mass media attention. Cherie Blair's involvement with cut-price mortgage arrangements and lifestyle consultants became Cheriegate; if a well-known character called Herbert had his unwholesome personal life made public, then that would become Herbertgate.

gazump MODPHEN a vocabulary item from the favourite and obsessive English pastime of house buying and selling; ***been bloody gazumped again, in' I?*** – *I have failed in my attempt at house purchase yet again as a result of the wretched seller accepting a higher bid than mine at the last minute, having previously accepted my own bid*

gazunder English housing being some of the most expensive in the world, buyers sometimes resort to underhand tactics. To gazunder is to lower your offer on a house just before you exchange contracts with the seller.

Gazza COLLOQUIAL a press name for Paul Gascoigne, a brilliant footballer some years back

GBH grievous bodily harm, a legalistic expression for *doing someone over*; *see that big gorilla over at the bar, well that's Dennis, been had up four times for GBH, right?*

GCHQ Government Communications Headquarters, the government's eavesdropping centre for gathering foreign intelligence

GCSE General Certificate of Secondary Education, the qualifications in individual subjects awarded to students after examination, generally at age 16; *he left school with no GCSEs at all – and look at him now*

geezer COLLOQUIAL a man, rather a downmarket word; *who's that geezer over by the door?; I bought it off a geezer I met down the pub*

Geordie COLLOQUIAL 1) a person from Newcastle; 2) of Newcastle; *a very strong Geordie accent*

get in → **I'll get 'em in** I'll buy a round of drinks; *come on Barry, it's your turn to get 'em in*

Gherkin, the the nickname – due to its shape – for one of the latest additions to the City skyline, the Swiss Re building, which won the Stirling prize for architecture in 2004

The Gherkin

glass ceiling MODPHEN the limit of promotion for women within an organization

Globe Theatre sited in Southwark, on the south bank of the Thames, and one of the main theatres in Elizabethan London, the original building saw many of the premieres of Shakespeare's plays. The reconstructed Globe opened in 1997, thanks to the titanic efforts of the American, Sam Wannamaker, and presents Shakespeare's plays in keeping with the way they were originally performed.

Glos Gloucestershire

Gloucester [pronounced gloster]

Glyndebourne seen by some as the quintessence of Englishness, a country-house setting for an annual opera festival where guests picnic and sip champagne on lush lawns before the show

go → don't pass go IDIOM don't collect any benefits; the reference is to the game of Monopoly® where, if you go to prison without passing go, you fail to pick up the standard £200 bonus

God slot COLLOQUIAL a time for a religious broadcast on TV

God squad COLLOQUIAL a mildly disparaging term for a fervent group of religious believers

Golden Brown COLLOQUIAL at the time of going to press, Chancellor of the Exchequer, Gordon Brown, bringer of gold and prosperity to the masses

🍽 **Golden Delicious** a popular type of apple

golden duck a batsman in cricket scores a golden duck when he is bowled out for no runs off the very first ball that he faces

golden handcuffs money offered to an employee, usually an executive, in order to induce him/her not to leave that job

golden handshake money given to an employee (an executive) on retirement or on being made redundant

golden hello money offered to an employee, usually an executive, in order to induce him/her to accept a job

golden parachute money an executive will receive if he/she loses his/her job as a result of a takeover or merger

Good Friday (Agreement) the agreement reached at Easter 1998 between the British and Irish governments on measures to restore parliamentary government in Northern Ireland

googly → **to throw someone a googly** IDIOM a googly in cricket is a ball which looks as though it's going to move one way, but in fact moves another way, so baffling the batsman; figuratively speaking, if you *throw someone a googly*, you hand them something which is very tricky to deal with

Goon Show an influential, somewhat surreal radio show from the 1950s, in a similar vein to **MONTY PYTHON** and much loved by Prince Charles. Jokes of the type – *he tore up the garden path* (sound of ripping paper) or *he fell into a heap on the ground – I don't know who left it there* – abound.

gor blimey SLANG a general exclamation of surprise; *500 quid? gor blimey!; look what they've gone and done to their house!, gor blimey, what a colour!*

gotcha COLLOQUIAL 1) got you, caught you; *come here you horrible dirty little spider you, gotcha!*; 2) got you, understood; *tomorrow morning, my place at 9.15, right gotcha*

goth COLLOQUIAL a goth is someone, generally young, who is inspired by heavy rock and dresses entirely and extravagantly in black with heavy make-up, with the result that they often look corpselike

Gradgrind the mill-owner in Charles Dickens' Hard Times, who was cold-hearted and only interested in facts; *the dreary laws of gradgrind economics*

grammar school a type of secondary school which assesses pupils on entry and puts them in different streams. Some grammar schools are now fee-paying.

grammar school boy a term loaded with class allusions; the grammar schools produce intelligent kids, but grammar schools are not public schools (hence lacking in something); *the new Minister, brilliant fellow, grammar school boy, isn't he?*

Grand National, the a major horse race, over fences, held every year at Aintree near Liverpool. The Grand National is especially well known because of the difficulty of the jumps. Usually only very few of the starters actually get to the finish and it is not uncommon to see horses finishing without their jockeys.

Granny Smith a type of sharp-tasting apple

Grauniad PRIVATE EYE's name for a national newspaper called THE GUARDIAN, which achieved fame for its misprints

Great War a name for the first World War; the second World War didn't get a special name; enough's enough

Green ink brigade COLLOQUIAL a jokey name for the often eccentric people who write pedantic, threatening or abusive letters to the media, politicians and celebrities

Green Paper the name for a parliamentary paper on a major topic for discussion and consultation before any legislation is contemplated

Green Wellie Brigade COLLOQUIAL an informal or contemptuous term for upper-class or COUNTY people who live in the country and wear Wellington boots and other outdoor gear to show off their status

🔊 **Greenwich** [pronounced grenitch]

Gretna Green a town just over the border in Scotland to which young people traditionally can elope if they want to get married without their parents' consent

🔊 **Grosvenor** [pronounced grove-ner]

gruesome twosome COLLOQUIAL two people who usually go together, though the expression can be said of two people who aren't really gruesome at all; *Bush and Blair, the gruesome twosome, stood behind their eagle lecterns smiling at the press; am I right in supposing that the gruesome twosome will be coming for Sunday lunch as usual?*

gsoh good sense of humour, usually found in the personal columns

Guardian, the a national newspaper known for its seriousness and leftwing views

Guardian-reader a type of person who will have leftwing views, be interested in and keen on talking about social and political matters and who is very probably middle class too

GUNPOWDER PLOT   85

Guards The Guards are among the most prestigious regiments in the British Army and carry out ceremonial duties for the monarch on state occasions. They mount guard at various palaces and have highly decorative uniforms. A guards' officer used to be considered the height of English gentlemanliness.

Guildford Four a celebrated case, the Guildford Four were three Irishmen and one Irishwoman imprisoned as the perpetrators of the Guildford bomb attacks in 1975 in which five people died and many were injured. Their conviction was quashed in 1989.

Y Guinness English only by adoption, a favourite with the Englishman or woman who prefers a slow, meditative beer, this Irish brand of stout, brewed in the very heart of Dublin, has become one of Ireland's most recognized brands worldwide

gully go to CRICKET

Gunners, the a nickname for Arsenal (football team)

Gunpowder Plot the failed plot in 1605 by Roman Catholic sympathizers to blow up the King in the Houses of Parliament

gutted COLLOQUIAL a modern term for disappointed, very upset; *England 2, Trinidad and Tobago 6, we were gutted*

guv COLLOQUIAL an informal yet grudgingly respectful way, primarily in the southeast, of addressing someone higher in the social pecking order than the speaker, a customer etc; *all right, guv, where do you want this settee put, then?*

guvnor COLLOQUIAL a respelling of *governor*, a way of addressing someone explained above, and written in this way to indicate the accent in which it's said

Guy Fawkes night 5th November, when effigies, known as Guys, of Guy Fawkes, the leader of the GUNPOWDER PLOT are burned on a bonfire and huge numbers of fireworks are let off. People don't always stick to the actual date of the 5th these days.

Guy's a London teaching hospital

H

🗣 **Hainault** [pronounced hay-nolt]

hair of the dog TRUNCID *a hair of the dog that bit you*; said when you think a small drink of what you drank buckets of the night before will help you start feeling better; *quick pint before lunch, Dave? – why not, hair of the dog, eh?*

half term English, and British, schools have a short holiday half way through each of the three school terms.

half-inch [RHYMING SLANG] to pinch, to steal; *some bugger's gone and half-inched me bike*

Hammers, the a nickname for West Ham football club

Hampstead an affluent area of north London once noted for being the home of many intellectuals, especially left-wing ones; *he's just another woolly-minded Hampstead liberal*

Hants Hampshire

happy hour [MODPHEN] In the early evening, this is when you can buy drinks in pubs at reduced prices. No connection with **BINGE-DRINKING**.

happy slapping [MODPHEN] Technology moves on and human nature stays relentlessly fixed. Teenagers can now attack and beat up another teenager, record the event on a mobile phone and send the gruesome pictures to friends and others. This is *happy slapping*.

happy-clappy At happy-clappy churches the congregation is encouraged to behave as though they were at a pop concert, generally let themselves go and do not feel obliged to sit sedately in their pews.

Hardy country refers to parts of Dorset lyrically described by the novelist Thomas Hardy in some of his novels

Harley Street a street associated with expensive doctors; *I went and got a top-class Harley Street opinion*

Harrods® a large and very upmarket department store in Knightsbridge

Harrovian an Old Harrovian is a former pupil of Harrow

Harrow a famous public school

Harvey Nicks COLLOQUIAL an abbreviation most likely to be used by a person who shops at Harvey Nichols, an upmarket department store for fashionable and designer goods

👂 **Harwich** [pronounced harritch]

Hatton Garden the traditional centre of the jewellery trade in Britain, near Holborn in London

hearts (of oak) RHYMING SLANG broke; *me lend you a tenner?, I'm arts meself, mate*

Heath Robinson COLLOQUIAL mechanically ingenious but complicated and weird-looking; *what do you think of my back-garden wind farm? – a bit Heath Robinson, but it works*

heave-ho → **to get the old heave-ho** COLLOQUIAL 1) to be sacked; 2) to be thrown out (by your wife/husband); 3) to be discarded; *time to give these 1998 future-proof PCs the old heave-ho*

> **Henley (Week)** Henley Royal Regatta started in 1839 and is an extremely prestigious annual rowing competition with its own rules held at Henley-on-Thames, near Oxford, with the monarch as patron. Henley week is in early July.

Henman Hill a grassy bank at Wimbledon where tennis matches can be watched on a large screen; the place has been rechristened MURRAY MOUNT

her indoors COLLOQUIAL the wife; the expression comes from an 80s TV programme called the Minder in which ARTHUR DALY had a wife who was never seen and who was mysteriously referred to as *her indoors*.

herbert SLANG a twit, an idiot; *everyone else could speak French and I felt a right herbert, I can tell you*

Herts Hertfordshire

High, the There are doubtless several of these, but the main reference is to the street in the centre of Oxford.

high street → **prices on the high street** an informal measure used to show how inflation is going, looking at prices in the major retail chains

> **high street bank** one of the small number of major banking chains

> **high street shops** a shorthand way of referring to the major chains of shops which are to be found in most English high streets

(making most of them mirror images of each other)

high tea a traditional late-afternoon meal, now rarely eaten, of tea, cakes and a cooked dish

Highway Code the rules that motorists and road users are meant to obey

Hillsborough a major peacetime disaster, and part of the English collective consciousness, in which 96 Liverpool football fans died after being crushed to death at the Hillsborough stadium in Sheffield in 1989

🗣 **Holborn** [pronounced ho-bn]

Holloway a London prison for women

home → **an Englishman's home** TRUNCID *an Englishman's home is his castle*; whatever its size, wherever it may be, the place you call home is the place where you are/should be entitled to please yourself and be king

Home Counties the counties around London: Berkshire, Buckinghamshire, Essex, Hertfordshire, Kent, Surrey and Sussex; they are seen as the natural home of Englishness

hon honourable 1) used in Parliament when one member refers to another; *as* *my honourable friend, the Minister for Trade, has pointed out*; 2) used in front of the titles of certain office-holders; *The Honourable Mr Justice Andrew Smith*; 3) a title given to the children of certain ranks of the aristocracy

honourable → **the honourable member for...** Usually capitalized. An obligatory veneer of politeness and respect required of those in parliamentary debate. An utterance like *As the Honourable Member for Croydon has claimed...* neutralizes any feelings the speaker may have for this particular MP.

honours an honours degree, which is the standard type of English undergraduate degree

Honours List the list of people, often volunteers, who are deemed to have made a significant contribution to public life and who will be honoured with a decoration such as an MBE. The list is published on the QUEEN'S BIRTHDAY and at New Year.

Hooray Henry COLLOQUIAL a loud and boisterously jolly upperclass young man (often to be spotted together with a SLOANE RANGER).

"hope springs eternal" the line is from Alexander Pope and has become a commonly used idiom; *he's been trying to get his novel published now for 15 years, hope springs eternal*

hot desking MODPHEN not having a fixed place of work, but carrying data electronically between various workstations in various locations; also a verb; *since he started to hotdesk it...*

House of Fraser® a major, somewhat upmarket, department store chain

HRH His/Her Royal Highness; *HRH will be doing the opening ceremony*

hundred historically, a subdivision of a county possessing its own court

I

Independent®, the a daily newspaper which prides itself on its high editorial standards and its lack of adherence to a single party-political viewpoint

Ingerland the name of England as sometimes chanted by football fans

innit COLLOQUIAL 1) a cockneyish version of *isn't it* at the end of a statement; *ain't 'alf 'ot, innit?*; 2) an all-purpose tag question, not necessarily relating to the verb *to be*; *they overcharged us on the drinks, innit?* (here standard English would have **didn't they?**)

Inns of Court the four very ancient legal bodies in London which train English barristers and call them to the bar

inside On a bus, if you sit *inside* you sit downstairs, the expression dating back to the days when the top deck was exposed to the elements.

Irish COLLOQUIAL If something is said to be *a bit Irish*, then it is seen as illogical or contradictory.

Iron Lady, the COLLOQUIAL a press name for Margaret Thatcher

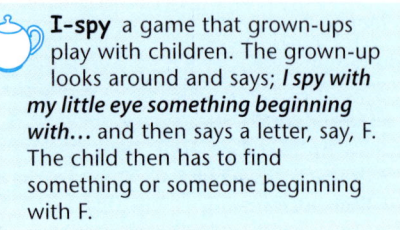

> **I-spy** a game that grown-ups play with children. The grown-up looks around and says; *I spy with my little eye something beginning with...* and then says a letter, say, F. The child then has to find something or someone beginning with F.

J

Jag a Jaguar, an upmarket and quintessentially British car, currently manufactured under German management

jamjar RHYMING SLANG car

Jekyll and Hyde If someone is described as being a bit of a Jekyll and Hyde, then that person has two sides to their character, one good and one evil. The reference is to a famous story by Robert Louis Stevenson, Dr Jekyll and Mr Hyde, in which the respectable Dr Jekyll would turn into the monstrous and evil Mr Hyde.

jellied eels pieces of eel, a COCKNEY delicacy which is now more traditional than actual; you'll still find them though

jimmy riddle RHYMING SLANG piddle, pee; *hang on love, gotta nip upstairs for a jimmy riddle*

joanna RHYMING SLANG piano; *in the days when we still had a singsong around the old joanna*

job → on the job SLANG having sex; *sorry mate, didn't know you was on the job, I'll call back later*

Jock COLLOQUIAL a Scotsman, humorous (or insulting)

Joe Bloggs COLLOQUIAL the ordinary person, the man-in-the-street; *democracy means that Joe Bloggs gets a say at elections but not afterwards*

Joe Soap the same as JOE BLOGGS

John Bull the traditional embodiment of Englishness, first established in the 18th century, said to be honest, bold and plain-dealing

John Lewis® a department store, has a well-known slogan: *never knowingly undersold*

jolly

> very; can be reasonably unexceptionable; ***they're jolly nice people; I should jolly well think so*** – but will always tend to the more upper middle-class type of usage; ***that's jolly unkind of you, Roger*** – and is a fairly standard piece of linguistic equipment for anyone wanting to mimic a posh, upper-class accent

jolly hockey sticks DATED used as an adjective to describe a girl or woman with a bluff, apparently carefree attitude, sporty and sporting and middle-class; ***really surprising how a quiet little mouse of a chap like Geoffrey would fall for someone like Caroline, she's so jolly hockey sticks***

Joneses Keeping up with the Joneses, making sure you are not outdone materially by your neighbours, became a catchphrase in Britain in the fifties and sixties; *keeping up with the Joneses has added to Britain's debt problem*

K

k [pronounced kay] means *thousand*; *she's on £45k – she earns £45,000 a year*

Kangaroo Valley DATED an old name for Earls Court in London, so called because of the large number of Australians living there

karzy a slightly dated slang and humorous way of referring to the toilet; *can't hold his beer, keeps going to the karzy every ten minutes*

kebab → to go for a kebab MODPHEN a latterly traditional post-pub activity, eating a kebab from a late-night takeaway

Ken (Livingstone) The famous and reforming Mayor of London is usually known (in the press) just by his Christian name, Ken.

> **kettle → to put the kettle on** to start making a cup of tea, indicating the start of a period of conversation and relaxation; *come on in, I'd just put the kettle on*

KG Knight of the Garter, the Order of the Garter being the highest and oldest order of English chivalry. Its members are chosen by the monarch and number only 25, including the sovereign.

Khyber RHYMING SLANG (the full form is *Khyber pass*) arse; ***he got a kick right up the Khyber***

King's Road A fashionable place to be and to shop in the SWINGING SIXTIES, this Chelsea street is still famous for its trendy shops.

knackered COLLOQUIAL 1) exhausted, tired out; 2) broken, no longer fit to use

knackeroonied SLANG a jokey distortion of KNACKERED, used mainly in the sense of *tired*.

knees-up COLLOQUIAL a party, a celebration, a dance

Knightsbridge an upmarket area of London

knockers SLANG breasts

knocking shop SLANG a brothel

Knowledge, the It sounds mystical, Zen. The Knowledge is the comprehensive exam on London's streets and landmarks that taxi-drivers have to pass before they can be licensed to work.

Kwik-fit® a garage workshop chain specializing in exhausts, tyres and shock absorbers

L

lad → **a bit of a lad** Calling a man a bit of a lad means he's a bit naughty, especially as regards having success with women; *you wouldn't think it to look at him now, but in his day Trevor was a bit of a lad*

laddish COLLOQUIAL a man described as laddish takes part in male activities such as sport, casual sex and heavy drinking and is possibly rather boorish and immature; *he goes in for a lot of laddish banter*

ladette COLLOQUIAL a woman who indulges in aspects of traditional male behaviour, ie drinking too much, being brash, loud and foul-mouthed, being on the pull; *binge-drinking has increased with the rise of the ladette*

Ladies' Day Ladies' Day at ASCOT is when the ladies come in all their finery, especially in elaborate and exotic headgear, which the press and media love to report on

lady and gent RHYMING SLANG rent; *that'll be Mrs Godfrey looking for the lady and gent*

Lady Godiva a very well-known English

folk heroine. Legend has it that she rode through Coventry naked in return for getting her husband to reduce the taxes he imposed on the citizens.

Lady Muck COLLOQUIAL a woman with inflated ideas of personal grandeur; *oh, so Lady Muck would like her bags taken up to her room for her, would she?*

lady of the lamp, the a nickname for FLORENCE NIGHTINGALE

lager a kind of light, effervescent beer which has only been widely drunk in England over the last thirty years or so. As it is lighter than traditional beers, more of it can be drunk before the effects are noticed.

lager lout COLLOQUIAL someone, especially a man, who engages in antisocial, unruly and probably crude behaviour while under the influence of beer

lager lovely COLLOQUIAL not a boozed-up stunner but one of the models formerly pictured on beer cans

lager top a lager beer with a small amount of lemonade or similar soft drink on top

Lake District an inspiration to the English Romantic movement in the 19th century – this picturesque national park

LAST NIGHT OF THE PROMS 101

of fells (hills) and lakes is one of the most popular tourist areas in Britain

Lambeth Palace the mainly Tudor residence of the Archbishop of Canterbury, the senior cleric in the Church of England. Lambeth Palace is in London.

Lancs Lancashire

> **Land of Hope and Glory** the opening line and title of a rather triumphalist anthem, with chest-swelling music by the ever so English Elgar, its words reflect English imperialism in its heyday. It is nowadays largely confined to the LAST NIGHT OF THE PROMS and the Conservative party.
>
> The first lines are:
>
>> Land of hope and glory
>> Mother of the free
>> How shall we extol thee
>> Who are born of thee?

Land of Nod sleep, in baby talk; *time to head off to the Land of Nod*

large brandy/whisky a large one is a double measure

last night of the Proms the closing night of the Promenade concerts or PROMS, in which the audience takes part with great gusto, especially in the patriotic song LAND OF HOPE AND GLORY which is a traditional part of the programme

last orders the time at which you can order your last drink in an English pub; *when's last orders, Charlie?*

lbw leg before wicket; in cricket a batsman will be out, dismissed, if a ball hits his leg and the umpires judges that the ball would have gone through to hit the wickets if the batsman's leg had not obstructed it

"lead on, Macduff" an invitation to another person to go first, to take the lead, the reference being to Shakespeare's Macbeth

> A: I think the hotel is along this street somewhere, Geoffrey
>
> B: if you say so, lead on, Macduff

leak → **to go for a leak** COLLOQUIAL to urinate; *I had to go out for a leak in the carpark*

"lean and hungry look (about him)" from Shakespeare's Julius Caesar, implies that the person referred to is seen as a threat

learned → **my learned friend** a lawyer's

way of referring to another lawyer in court, it implies nothing as to real friendship

lech lech an utterance signifying distaste at someone's sexual interest; *look at him staring at Julie, lech lech, the dirty old bugger*

leg (side) the side of a cricket field to the left of a righthanded batsman's legs

leg break a ball that the bowler spins from leg to OFF

Lego® a children's construction kit consisting of brightly coloured interlocking plastic parts

🄳 **Leics** [pronounced less] Leicestershire

🄳 **Leicester** [pronounced lester]

licensing hours the times of day or night when it is legal for pubs and bars to sell alcohol

Licensing Laws the laws controlling when, where and to whom it is legal to sell alcohol

lifestyle consultant MODPHEN a person who, in return for a fee, advises and assists another in their daily life, helping them shop and choose clothes, helping them with a personal fitness routine etc

🍸 **light (ale)** a type of bottled beer which is low in hop and alcohol content

like → I was like

> This is a new(ish) way of saying *I said*; *I was like you can't be serious!* But it has the advantage of being able to refer to non-verbal reactions as well. So: *I was like...* (followed by contorted face displaying total incomprehension) is a way of saying *I didn't have the slightest idea as to what might be meant*.

limerick

> All Brits love a good limerick and a lot of people like making them up, for laughs. Here's a typical example of the limerick format:
>
> *A young ballet dancer from Ealing*
> *Once knocked herself out on the ceiling*
> *Her partner asked why*
> *If she must leap so high*
> *Could she not show more neighbourly feeling.*

Lincs Lincolnshire

🍽 **liquid lunch** a drink in the pub at lunchtime rather than some food; or maybe a little food with a drink or two

listed If a building is *listed* then it is registered (and protected) as being of special historical or architectural interest.

lit crit literary criticism

little black book more likely to take the form of a mobile or an organizer nowadays, a notebook in which people, generally men, keep girlfriends' phone numbers

little Englander COLLOQUIAL some who thinks that everything English is the best in the world

little lord Fauntleroy a child whose behaviour is so perfect as to be nauseating

Liverpudlian 1) from Liverpool; 2) a person from Liverpool

load → **what a load of...** TRUNCID Often left incomplete (though it could be finished off with *rubbish*, *bollocks* etc), this signifies contempt, disbelief and rejection.

☗ **local** The locals (or people who live locally) often meet at the local (or local pub).

lollipop lady, lollipop man a lady or man who stops the traffic for children on their way to or from school

London Orbital, the the M25

long → **it's a long road** TRUNCID things won't stay bad indefinitely, something will change, something will turn up; from the full saying *it's a long road that has no turning*, ie every road will eventually change direction at some point

long-off go to CRICKET

long-on go to CRICKET

Lonsdale Belt a prize for boxing

loo the commonest word for the toilet

loony left the left wing of a party, whose ideas are thought to be crazy and out of touch with reality

Lord Muck COLLOQUIAL the male equivalent to LADY MUCK; *look at him, sitting there like Lord Muck in the best armchair*

Lord's one of the country's main cricket grounds; this one is in north London, not to be confused with…

Lords, the the Upper Chamber of the Houses of Parliament

🍸 lounge (bar) the part of a pub with upholstered seats, a carpet and slightly higher prices (compare: PUBLIC BAR)

love a friendly way to address someone, used by men to women or women to men; *can I help you, love? you look a bit lost*

love → my love a way of addressing someone similar to *love*, can sound even more alarmingly personal – although it isn't; *could you just park your car over by the fence, my love*

L-plate learner drivers have to display L-plates to show that they are still learning

LSD SLANG as well as the drug, this can mean *money*; it comes from the old system of pounds, shillings and pence, the old abbreviation for a penny being d

ltr long-term relationship, as sought in lonely-hearts columns

Luddite opposed to the changes brought about by technology on working life

Lunchtime O'Booze the name of a (fictional) journalist who writes for **PRIVATE EYE**

luv(v)a duck DATED COLLOQUIAL expresses surprise or displeasure; *luva duck, June me old girl, do you think I'm made of money!*

luvvly-jubbly COLLOQUIAL a jokey expression of pleasure

luvvy SLANG a disparaging term for an actor, especially an actor who acts like an actor when not actually acting; *the award, to the dismay of all the assembled luvvies, went to a rank outsider and new boy*

M

Macca a press name for Paul McCartney (ex-Beatle)

mad dogs and Englishmen TRUNCID *mad dogs and Englishmen go out in the midday sun*; from a Noel Coward song; the English have a way of ignoring presumably sensible local habits and carrying on with their own way of life, wherever they may be; or just: the English are intrepid;

> A: *fancy a local brandy?*
> B: *why not, mad dogs and Englishmen*

Maggie Margaret Thatcher

Magna Carta meaning *the great charter*, granted by King John in 1215 to his rebellious barons and setting out their rights and those of the church and freemen. Magna Carta is traditionally seen as the forerunner of British democratic practice.

maiden over In cricket when a bowler bowls his six deliveries (an over) without a batsman managing to score a run off him, that is called a *maiden over*. This has generated the hoary clichéd pun that is embedded in every English psyche and is guaranteed to make every mother's son blush; *he's bowled his first maiden over.*

Mail®, the (short for the Daily Mail) a national tabloid newspaper of firmly populist views

maisonette a type of flat occupying two floors of a larger building. Distinguished from a duplex by being more traditional and more English.

Mall, the the wide avenue running from Trafalgar Square to Buckingham Palace [pronounced to rhyme with pal]

Man Booker Prize same as the BOOKER PRIZE

Mancunian 1) a person from Manchester; 2) from Manchester

M&S an affectionate nickname for MARKS AND SPENCER'S

ManU Manchester United, one of England's top football teams

Marks & Sparks COLLOQUIAL a nickname for Marks and Spencer's

Marks & Spencer's the well-known department store chain. Such is the affection of the British public for this shop that its financial and trading fortunes and misfortunes are frequently broadcast on the national news.

Mary Whitehouse She was famous for leading a campaign against the use of foul language and the portrayal of sex and violence in the media.

🔊 **Marylebone** [pronounced marlee-bone]

Matchbox toys® a hugely popular series of miniature replicas of cars, first made in the early 1950s and so named because, being less than three inches in length, they could fit inside a large matchbox

mate COLLOQUIAL a friendly (usually) way of addressing another man; *you got the time, mate?*

May Ball Held in June, the fittingly named May Balls are lavish all-night festivities in **OXBRIDGE** colleges. They celebrate the end of the academic year.

Mayfair an upmarket area of central London

MBE Member of the British Empire, an honour awarded in the **HONOURS LIST** for public service

MCC the governing body of English cricket (the initials stand for Marylebone Cricket Club – which is of no relevance)

me

> very commonly used in place of *my*, just an informal (but not downmarket) usage: *this is the pocket I keep me money in*

MERC 111

meals on wheels the provision of cooked meals to the elderly or housebound; *she organized meals on wheels for the Red Cross for many years*

mean → know what I mean? A common filler which, although it can be meaningful; (said with a wink) *he's working late tonight, know what I mean?* is more often than not totally devoid of meaning; *well, I like lasagne, know what I mean?*

🍽 **meat and two veg** 1) the traditional standard English meal; *rice, pizza, pasta... at least once a week we should have meat and two veg*; 2) a man's genitals

Meccano® a classic children's toy, consisting of metal and plastic components, enabling mechanically-minded children to create their own machines, engines and fantastic contraptions, now replaced by LEGO®

Mekon the iconic evil enemy of the comic-strip hero DAN DARE in THE EAGLE. A green-tinged, Venusian with an enormous, bulbous skull housing a vast brain, he is emotionless, totally evil, and bent on world domination.

Merc [pronounced murk] a Mercedes

Merlin the magician at the court of KING ARTHUR

Merry Men the band of men who teamed up with ROBIN HOOD

Met Office the Meteorological Office, the coordinating body for weather prediction, not to be confused with the following, the MET

Met, the the Metropolitan Police, London's main police force

mews Mews are a type of housing found mainly in London and are the converted stables, usually in a row, at the back of larger houses. They are highly sought after and very expensive.

MFI® a store famous for (reasonably) low-price furniture, a lot of which is self-assembly

M4 corridor The M4 heads west out of London bound for Slough, Maidenhead and Reading. Along its hard shoulders and slip roads lie centres of largely IT and IT-related industry. This is the M4 corridor, a swathe of high tech and high prices.

Mick COLLOQUIAL a disparaging term for an Irishman

Middle England not a place but a genus, Middle England is made up of ordinary Englishmen and women, who are not extreme in their attitudes, who have ordinary aspirations, who are probably quite conservative in outlook and who live outside of London; *do politicians follow what Middle England thinks or do they shape this?*

middle name If you say that X is your middle name, then you mean that you are famous for X; *punctuality is not exactly Fiona's middle name*

Midlands, the the area around Birmingham, traditionally known for industry

mid-off go to CRICKET

mid-on go to CRICKET

mid-wicket go to CRICKET

MI5 [pronounced em-eye-five] the old name, but the one which is still generally used, for the British government Security Service, responsible for internal security and counterintelligence within Britain

Mike → **for the love of Mike** COLLOQUIAL an expression of exasperation; *for the love of Mike, what did you do that for?*

🍸 **mild** a light-bodied, mildly-hopped beer

mile high club MODPHEN 'club' of all those people who have had sex a mile up in an airplane; there's no waiting list to join

Millennium Bridge, the a new pedestrian-only bridge built to celebrate the new millennium. It is mainly famous for its initial structural problems. Heavy foot traffic on its first day of use caused worrying movements that led to its being closed for structural alterations. It has since become known as the Wibbly Wobbly Bridge.

Millennium Dome, the a large building put up by government funding to house an exhibition to celebrate the start of the new millennium. The Dome failed to live up to expectations and became a symbol of misspent public money.

Millennium Stadium, the a big, brand-new sports arena in Cardiff, used for international rugby and football matches (famous for its roof that closes right over to keep out the rain)

mince pies [RHYMING SLANG] eyes; *you keep yer mince pies off of her, you dirty old bugger, you*

minicab a taxi which has to be booked (by going to an office or by phoning) and which can't be stopped on the street

Minnie the Minx a legendary female character from THE BEANO, famous for being stronger than the boys, mischievous and cheeky

Mirror®, the shorthand for the Daily Mirror, a pictorial and populist newspaper

MI6 [pronounced em-eye-six] the old name, but the one still used, for the Secret Intelligence Service, which engages in security and espionage overseas to protect British interests

mockney

> 1) exaggerated or false COCKNEY diction; 2) a Mockney is a person who talks like a Cockney

"mock not" don't mock. The old English grammar re-emerged fossilized in this line originating in a TV programme about old Pompeii.

Mondeo Man COLLOQUIAL 1) the archetypal, mid-income man, probably with working-class roots, now doing well in white-collar land; 2) this man and his family, identified by pollsters as an electoral group

Monster Raving Loony Party a political party set up to satirize established political parties, it fields candidates and consistently wins a small number of votes at general elections

Monty Python a TV comedy programme that continued and reinforced the English love of the absurd. Among the famous sketches, which have entered the English psyche, are the *Ministry of Silly Walks* and the *Dead Parrot Sketch*.

Moors, the Yorkshire a large area of high, open countryside with sparse vegetation. Generally the Moors are associated with wildness, freedom, quaint rustic villages and romantic heroes and heroines. They are a paradise for walkers and nature lovers.

morning → **looking like the morning after** TRUNCID *looking like the morning after the night before* looking absolutely terrible, as though you have been up partying all night

> **Morris dancing** a traditional, stylized form of English country dancing performed in the open air. The dancers dress mainly in white, have small bells attached to them, and often wave handkerchiefs. Morris dancing is strictly for men only.

MOT [pronounced em-o-tee] the roadworthiness test that vehicles must pass in order to be legally used on the roads

mother → **some mothers do 'ave 'em!** IDIOM an exclamation of exasperation at a person's stupidity or incompetence

mother's ruin RHYMING SLANG gin

motorway madness MODPHEN collective motoring insanity; *8 dead in motorway madness pileup on fogbound M6*

Mousetrap, the London's longest running theatrical production, an Agatha Christie whodunnit first performed in 1952 and now part of the London sights

M25 the motorway which encircles the whole of the London area, planned as a fast way of getting from A to B, now famous for being nearly always heavily congested

"much ado about nothing" from the name of a play by Shakespeare, a lot of fuss about something which turns about to be trivial; *they held a full enquiry, but it was all much ado about nothing*

mucker → **me old mucker** DATED SLANG my old friend; *Bobby, me old mucker, lend us a tenner, there's a pal*

muggins DATED COLLOQUIAL a fool, a twerp; *what muggins left the window open then?* But also used for disparaging self-reference; *of course, muggins here (ie me) had to believe that she really meant it when she said she loved me*

muggle SLANG a word from the Harry Potter books for someone who has no skill in a particular activity and is excluded from the group that describes them as a *muggle*

Murray Mount the new name for a grassy bank at Wimbledon where tennis matches can be watched on a large screen, the name will doubtless change as new heroes emerge (Murray Mount for Andrew Murray having ousted Henman Hill for Tim Henman)

mush SLANG a southern, rather downmarket, way of addressing someone, with the letter u pronounced as in *push*; *are you staring at me, mush?*

must

> a newish prefix for verbs, turning them into adjectives;
> *a must-have fashion accessory;*
> *the main must-see buildings;*
> *one of the must-try wines*

mutt and jeff RHYMING SLANG deaf

mystery tour a trip to an unknown destination, often with a historical or ghostly twist

N

national insurance number the number issued to every person in the UK. NI contributions taken from employees and employers are used by the state to fund health care, care of the elderly and unemployment benefits.

negative equity MODPHEN When the value of the property on which you have taken out a mortgage is actually less than the amount of the mortgage to be repaid then you can be said to be suffering from *negative equity*. Greedy Brits are easily encouraged to take out huge loans to buy pokey little houses in the expectation that the value of the house will shoot up and make them rich when they sell it. An Englishman's home is an investment opportunity.

never knowingly undersold the motto of the major department store chain John Lewis, who promise to refund the difference between the price they charge for an item and a lower price in any other shop

New Forest an area in Hampshire of ancient, formerly royal, forest and now a nature reserve, popular with outdoor types, especially riders

> **New Labour** Tony Blair's name for the Labour party that came to power in 1997. Some say that New Labour is a dressed-up version of old Tory.

New Man MODPHEN a type of man who is in touch with the gentler side of his nature, rejects stereotyped male roles, and does an equal share of childcare and housework

🍸 **Newkie Brown** COLLOQUIAL a colloquial name for Newcastle Brown®, a sweetish beer

newt → **like the proverbial newt** IDIOM drunk (because there is an idiom *as drunk as a newt*)

> **NHS** National Health Service, the organization set up in 1948 to provide equal, free health care for everyone, reform of which is a major (but intractable) political issue, since clearly the better the NHS becomes the greater the number of problems it will create for itself

NI NATIONAL INSURANCE

Nice Guy → **no more Mr Nice Guy** IDIOM I'm going to get tough, you had better watch out

"nice to see ya – to see ya nice" a catchphrase associated with the veteran comedian and quiz show presenter, Bruce Forsyth

nick SLANG police station; *they took him down the nick*

nicker SLANG a pound; never in the plural; not a very posh word to use; *it cost me two hundred and twenty nicker*

night → **it'll be all right on the night** IDIOM The main reference is to theatrical productions, the implication being that problems will be sorted out by the time of the first performance. But this is also said generally to reassure someone that things will be ok when it matters.

nimby not in my back yard; *we're actually very much in favour of a recycling facility around here, but don't think our street is perhaps quite the best place to site it – that's the attitude of a nimby*

🍽 **99** [pronounced ninety-nine] A 99 is an ice-cream cone with a bar of flaky chocolate stuck into the ice cream.

999 [pronounced nine nine nine] the emergency number to dial for fire, police or ambulance

1966 A date which the English recall with nostalgia and pride, when, 900 years after being invaded by the French, in the famous year of 1066, the nation had developed to produce a football team which defeated Germany to win the World Cup.

nineteenth hole IDIOM the bar or clubhouse, in golfing contexts

NME New Musical Express, a very influential pop music magazine

no way José COLLOQUIAL definitely not; José is just there to make a rhyme and stress the point; *£500? no way José*

nob COLLOQUIAL an informal word for someone who is posh or upper-class; *then all the nobs go off and have their champagne on the lawn*

noble → **my noble friend** the term by which members of The House of Lords refer to each other in debates in The House

non-scene referring to a gay person who does not frequent the gay scene

Nora Batty a bad-tempered old woman (with sagging stockings), a character in a popular TV programme called Last of the Summer Wine

Northants Northamptonshire

not

> can be put, all on its own, at the end of a statement, after a slight pause, to negate all the preceding:
> *that was the best birthday party I have ever had – not*

Notting Hill Carnival an annual carnival organized by the Afro-Caribbean community in London's Notting Hill area. It features bands, floats and colourful costumes and is immensely popular with Londoners.

Notts Nottinghamshire

noughties, the COLLOQUIAL We looked back at the seventies, eighties and nineties but were, for a time, stumped as to what call the years from 2000 onwards. But are the noughties really naughty?

November 5th the date of the annual BONFIRE NIGHT

n/s short for NON-SCENE

nudge nudge IDIOM also heard as *nudge, nudge, wink, wink*, a catchphrase from MONTY PYTHON used as a way of introducing or following up a suggestive remark; *nudge, nudge, wink, wink, I've never seen him out with his wife*

Number 11 not as commonly used as Number 10, the nextdoor neighbour's number is used to refer to the Chancellor of the Exchequer

Number 10 1) the London home of he Prime Minister; *he was called around to Number 10*; 2) the Prime Minister; *what will Number 10 have to say about this?*

OFFICIAL SECRETS ACT

NVQ National Vocational Qualification, a qualification in a practical skill which is achieved at work

O

O level ordinary level, the old name for the exams in school subjects taken at around the age of 15-16, and now replaced by GCSE

OBE Officer of the (Order of the) British Empire, an honour ranking below an **MBE** award in the **HONOURS LIST**

Observer®, the the world's first Sunday newspaper, slightly left of centre and upmarket

odds and sods IDIOM miscellaneous things or people; *I've still got a few odds and sods left over*

Ofcom The Office of Telecommunications, the independent body which monitors and regulates the telecommunications industry

off (side) the side of the field to the righthand side of a righthanded batsman

Official Secrets Act If you sign the Official Secrets Act you undertake not to reveal to unauthorized persons anything about your work or the information to which you have access.

offie COLLOQUIAL off-licence, a shop that sells alcohol

off-spinner a bowler who uses off spin, a type of spin which directs the ball to the OFF SIDE

Ofsted The Office for Standards in Education, the independent body whose job is to monitor and maintain teaching standards in schools through regular inspections

Ofwat The Office of Water Services, the independent body which monitors and regulates the water industry

oh no he isn't! IDIOM the standard reply to this is: *oh yes he is!*; the reference being to PANTOMIMES

> A: *the monster's right behind you!*
> B: *oh no he isn't!*
> entire audience: *oh yes he is!*

OHMS On Her/His Majesty's Service

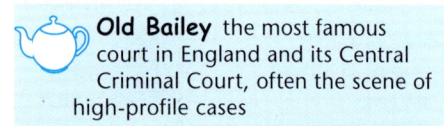

> **Old Bailey** the most famous court in England and its Central Criminal Court, often the scene of high-profile cases

old Bill, the SLANG the police

OLDE WORLDE

Old Lady of Threadneedle Street, the the Bank of England

> **old school tie** People who go to the same school, especially a prestigious public school, are rumoured to help each other by wielding influence, often at the expense of talent. The school tie is their badge of identity; *I wrongly these old school tie types had all died out*

Old Trafford 1) a famous cricket ground in Manchester; 2) the home ground of Manchester United football team

Old Vic, the the name by which everyone knows the Royal Victoria Theatre, one of the most famous theatres in London, near Waterloo Station

> **old-boy network** the supposed group of people who went to the same school or university and help each other obtain jobs, contracts and other benefits; *there's still very much an old-boy network in The City*

olde worlde COLLOQUIAL [pronounced oldee worldee] made up to look as though it belongs to a previous age; *a restaurant with oak beams, an open fire and a generally olde worlde feel*

one

> 1) an impersonal way of referring to people in general (quite a formal way of talking; *you* is the more frequently used alternative in the following); *if one drinks too much, one's sure to put on weight*; 2) a very posh way of referring to yourself, supposedly used by royalty; *one is really rather fed up with all these reporters chasing one all the time*

one hundred and eighty! the cry that goes up when three darts land on the treble 20 in darts; this is the highest score possible with a single throw of three darts

one man's meat TRUNCID *one man's meat is another man's poison*; people have different tastes and that has to be accepted

o.n.o. or nearest offer (as used in for sale ads)

oopsa-daisy COLLOQUIAL said when someone 1) almost or actually falls; 2) drops something; 3) is being picked up again (like a toddler that has stumbled)

Open University the largest university in Britain, where students without academic qualifications can study part-time, mainly through distance-learning

Ordnance Survey the organization responsible for surveying and map-making. Ordnance Survey maps are regarded as standards.

Other → **A N Other**

> used to refer to a person, whose name is not known or whose identity is not established or can be used to stand for any unspecified individual

other → **a bit of the other** IDIOM as vague-sounding as you can get, but it means specifically *sex*, probably getting a bit dated now though; *I'll tell you what's good for high blood pressure? a bit of the other*

OTT COLLOQUIAL over the top, exaggerated; *a £500 penalty was a bit OTT; the media's reaction was completely OTT*

OU OPEN UNIVERSITY

"out damned spot!" from Shakespeare's Macbeth, said by Lady Macbeth when she cannot remove the bloodstain from her hand after convincing Macbeth to kill Duncan; *will nothing get this red wine stain off the rug!, out damned spot!*

Oval, the one of the most famous cricket grounds in England, situated in south London

owzat Derived from *how's that?*, this is the shout you'll hear from cricketers when they claim that a batsman is out. In a non-sport sense it can be used, and is used particularly by the press, as a headline, implying that a person is finished, done for.

> **Oxbridge** There's no such place. England's two most prestigious universities, Oxford and Cambridge, are known jointly as Oxbridge; *what percentage of the House of Lords come from Oxbridge?*

Oxon A B.A. (Oxon) is a B.A. from Oxford University.

Oyster card a travel card for London transport

Oz COLLOQUIAL 1) Australia; 2) Australian (language, adjective, but not the person, who is an Ozzie)

P

p penny or pence; so you can say 1p or 50p; never in the plural though; *let's not worry about a couple of p*

Paddy COLLOQUIAL an Irishman, humorous (or insulting)

page three the page where the SUN will have a picture of a girl with big boobs

page three girl a girl who poses topless on page three of the SUN; *from page 3 girl to supermodel in two easy steps*

Paki COLLOQUIAL an offensive name for 1) a person from Pakistan or, since slang can be sloppy, from India or Bangladesh; 2) a small local shop run by Pakistanis (or Indians)

🍽 **pakora** a staple part of 'Indian' food in Britain, it consists of small portions of vegetables, meat, or fish coated in spicy batter, deep-fried and eaten as a starter

Palace, the Buckingham Palace; the Queen (or King); *how is the Palace going to react to all this?* – not to be confused with Palace without the word *the*, which is short for Crystal Palace, a London football team

Pancake Day Shrove Tuesday, when traditionally people eat pancakes.

panto short for PANTOMIME

> **pantomime** traditional theatrical entertainment for children around the Christmas holidays, loosely based on classic children's stories like Cinderella or Aladdin. There will always be a PRINCIPAL BOY (played by a girl) and an ugly old DAME (played by a man).

park and ride MODPHEN To help reduce inner-city congestion: you park your car in a special car park outside of the town centre and then a bus comes and collects you and takes you into the centre; *use the park and ride, it'll save time*

Parkhurst a men's prison on the Isle of Wight

PC Plod a jokey name for a policeman, implying a lack of intelligence; *well honestly darling, PC Plod kept me waiting for absolutely hours until he'd checked all through the boot*

Pearly King part of London folklore, particularly in the East End, a man who dresses in the pearly costume for special occasions and for charity. The costume consists of a suit and hat densely covered with patterns sewn with mother-of-pearl buttons

Pearly Queen the wife of the Pearly King, who also dresses in a pearly costume as described above

penny → **a penny for them** TRUNCID *a penny for your thoughts*; what is going through your mind?, said in a humorous way to someone who has fallen silent and stopped taking part in a conversation

penny → **in for a penny** TRUNCID *in for a penny, in for a pound*; starting something should imply a commitment to seeing it finished

Pete → **for Pete's sake** COLLOQUIAL just an emphasizer, no religious or other overtones; *but she's my sister, for Pete's sake!*

Peter Pan 1) a man who never seems to get older; 2) a man who never seems to grow up

Peter Principle, the If you are good at your job, you will be promoted until you reach a level at which you are no longer competent to do the job.

Petticoat Lane in the East End of London, a street famous for its Sunday morning market

P45 the form from the Inland Revenue issued by an employer to an employee who is leaving a job. *To get your P45* means to be fired; *I think I'll be getting my P45 soon*

Phil the Greek COLLOQUIAL a jocular name for the Duke of Edinburgh

phishing MODPHEN the attempt to get hold of another person's banking details, internet passwords etc in order to steal that person's money

Piccadilly Circus → **it's like Piccadilly Circus here** IDIOM it's extremely busy here, a lot of people moving around

piddle a mild and humorous word for *pee*; *I needed a piddle in the middle of Act 2*

pig's ear 1) RHYMING SLANG beer; *fancy a pint of pigs*; 2) IDIOM *to make a pig's ear of something* to make a mess of a job

pigs might fly IDIOM If someone says to you; *I just saw a pig fly past the window* – then they are implying that what you have just said is completely unrealistic and totally unlikely to happen. The reference is to the idiom *pigs might fly.*

pint The classic symbol of English pub life, the pint has so far resisted all attempts at metrication. If someone says to you: *fancy a pint?* this may be an invitation to do just that, drink a pint, but it may also be a lot more, an invitation to have a couple of drinks and share some conversation – relaxed, serious, intimate, personal, jovial or whatever.

PJs pyjamas

Plaistow [pronounced play-stoe]

plateglass A plateglass university is a modern university, especially one founded in the 1960s.

plates of meat RHYMING SLANG feet; *get yer dirty great plates of meat off me new covers*

ploughman's lunch a pub standard:

cheese, pickles and a hunk of bread; the expression is often abbreviated to *ploughman's*

plumbing → **I'll just go and inspect the plumbing** COLLOQUIAL I need to go to the toilet

Plymouth Hoe on the seafront at Plymouth, a spot made famous by Sir Francis Drake who was playing bowls there one day and, when told that the Spanish Armada had been sighted, calmly decided to finish his game of bowls before pressing the panic button

pocket billiards COLLOQUIAL If someone is playing pocket billiards then he is fingering his testicles with his hands in his pockets.

Poets' Corner not a place for readings, this is a part of Westminster Abbey where some famous English poets and writers are buried and where some have memorials

point go to CRICKET

point Percy SLANG short for *to point Percy at the porcelain*, a jokey expression for having a pee

poke a bit of sex; *I got a quick poke in the back seat*

Pompey Portsmouth, especially its football team; the name is never used with *the*.

pony SLANG £25; *it cost me a pony, nah, tell a lie, 35 quid*

pork pie RHYMING SLANG lie; *I think you've been telling some naughty little pork pies about us, mate*

porkie short for rhyming slang PORK PIE for lie

Portobello Road a street market in west London famous for its antique bric-a-brac and clothes

Posh Posh Spice alias Victoria Beckham

"pound of flesh" from Shakespeare's Merchant of Venice; a demand which someone is, strictly speaking, entitled to push for but which, in the opinion of most people, would be better forgotten; *he did me a really big favour five years ago – and now he wants his pound of flesh*

pounds, shillings and pence IDIOM British currency no longer has shillings, but this expression lives on: *I look after the customers and she keeps an eye on the pounds, shillings and pence*

poverty trap MODPHEN People get caught in the poverty trap when their income increases so as to be just above the minimum level at which they can receive government suppport.

preggers COLLOQUIAL pregnant

prep school a private school for youngsters who are not yet old enough to go to PUBLIC SCHOOL, short for preparatory school

presenteeism MODPHEN the opposite of absenteeism, presenteeism means maintaining an enormous and exaggeratedly long presence at one's place of employment in order to impress the bosses

Prezza COLLOQUIAL a press name for John Prescot, once a deputy prime minister

principal boy one of the main characters in a traditional PANTOMIME, played by an actress not an actor

Principality, the Wales

> **Private Eye®** a weekly magazine which is famous for its satire, wit and bold exposure of dishonest dealings

pro-choice MODPHEN in favour of the availability of abortion

pro-life MODPHEN opposed to the legal availability of abortion and to abortion as such

Proms an annual series of nightly concerts organized by the BBC and where part of the audience – the promenaders – stands. It runs through the height of the summer at the Royal Albert Hall and features some of the world's leading orchestras and soloists.

property ladder [MODPHEN] If you're on the property ladder, that means that you own a house or a flat, usually by means of having taken out a mortgage. It is the aspiration of most to get onto the property ladder so as to be able to spend a vast proportion of income in repaying the mortgage loan.

Pseud's Corner The satirical magazine, PRIVATE EYE, prints a weekly selection of pretentious bits of writing. So, if something written is described as being *a bit Pseud's Corner* that means it is trying too hard to be deep and has ended up being ridiculous.

P60 the annual statement issued by the Inland Revenue showing your tax status

🍽 **pub grub** food as served in a pub

🍸 **public bar** drinks will be slightly cheaper, the seats harder and the floor less carpeted than in the LOUNGE BAR

public school A public school is the same as a private school, the opposite of a state school. If someone is described as being *very public school* this means that they speak in an upper-class way.

Pudsey a teddy bear, with a spotted handkerchief over one eye, mascot of the BBC's annual fundraising event for children's charities

pull the other one (it's got bells on) IDIOM I don't believe you, don't try to kid me

pun The pun has become a national institution and has been passed down, as a tool, from comedian to adman to headline writer. Newspapers and magazines pun at the slightest opportunity; some can have no headline which is not a pun, for instance a critical review of clothes drying equipment might be headed; ***tumble dryers in a spin***

Q

QPR Queen's Park Rangers, a London football team

> **Queen's birthday, the** The Queen (or reigning monarch) has two birthdays: the actual and the official. The latter can fall on any of the first three Saturdays in June.

Queen's English, the

> the feminine version of The King's English, the correct, standard English to which people used to aspire, but which is now seen as old-fashioned and even élitist:
> ***the problem is, a lot of the new arrivals don't even understand the Queen's English***

> **Question Time** There are two of these. One is a regular session in the House of Commons. The other is a TV programme that struggles

> towards analytical debate while airing popular opinions.

quid pound; never used in the plural; *50 quid a ticket?*

R

R → **the three Rs** reading, writing and arithmetic are the three Rs that everybody agrees educationalists should concentrate on

RADA [pronounced rah-da], the Royal Academy of Dramatic Art, a famous London-based school for training actors

Radio Times the oldest established TV listings magazine, started by the BBC and a bit of an institution

rag and bone man There are very probably none left in modern Britain. A rag and bone man would go around houses collecting rubbish, old bits of broken equipment, old clothes etc – a precursor of recycling.

rage MODPHEN

> Rage has become a new suffix, used to describe the violent and uncontrolled behaviour of modern man when faced with a situation that causes frustration to

142 RANELAGH

> pass boiling point. Common examples are **AIR RAGE** for air passengers who feel upset that they are not allowed drunkenly and violently to abuse fellow passengers and crews, and **ROAD RAGE** for drivers who expect traffic jams to miraculously fade away and leave them alone on the open road. The suffix can be freely used: a computer which freezes might cause PC-rage, a defrosting refrigerator fridge rage.

Ranelagh [pronounced ran-luh]

read (at university) to study; *she went to Sussex and read law* – she studied law at Sussex University

real ale any beer allowed to ferment in the cask and served without added carbon dioxide. There is a vigorous campaign to support it.

Red Arrows 1) a group of formation-flying pilots in the Royal Air Force; 2) their red fighter jets

redbrick A redbrick university is one which was founded in the late 19th or early 20th century.

> **Red Nose Day** a day organized by **COMIC RELIEF** when people do a variety of stunts so as to raise

money for children's charities. To take part you have to wear a plastic stick-on nose.

red route a network of roads where parking is either completely banned or severely restricted, marked by a double red line at the side of the road

red tops the tabloid press

rhyming slang

Take a word pair or short phrase in which the last word rhymes with the word you want to refer to – and you have a rhyming slang equivalent. Some rhyming slang has just about passed into ordinary usage:

time to pay the lady and gent = time to pay the rent
a nice cup of Rosie Lee = a nice cup of tea.

Sometimes, to increase the complexity of the reference, the second part of the rhyming slang expression, the part that actually contains the rhyme, can be omitted:

to keep her Barnet dry = *to keep her Barnet Fair dry* = to keep her hair dry
he was on the dog to Leanne = *he was on the dog and bone to Leanne* = he was on the phone to Leanne

> Rhyming slang terms can also be invented more or less ad hoc, often disrespectfully playing on a well-known person's name. For example, assuming the existence of a well-known person called Brian Bragg:
>
> *he was upstairs having a Brian Bragg = he was upstairs having a Brian* = he was upstairs having a shag

Rich Tea® type of plain, dry biscuit, good for dunking in tea

Right Honourable a title put before their names when referring to certain ranks of the aristocracy, a Privy Councillor, an appeal-court judge, or the Lord Mayor of some cities

Ripper 1) Jack the Ripper, a notorious Victorian murderer who brutally mutilated the bodies of prostitutes in London's East End; 2) The Yorkshire Ripper, a serial killer in the seventies and eighties who similarly brutally murdered prostitutes

road → **one for the road** IDIOM a final drink before heading off home

road rage MODPHEN traffic-induced, other-motorist-induced uncontrollable anger, usually venting itself in physical violence

rob → **we was robbed** IDIOM a traditional claim in outrage at having lost a match, usually a football match, as a result of an unfair decision or possibly just a lucky goal for the other side

Robin Hood a legendary folk hero from the Middle Ages who lived in Nottingham forest and stood up for the rights of the poor; *they see their local councillor as a bit of a latter-day Robin Hood*

Roedean a well-known public school for girls

Roller COLLOQUIAL a Rolls Royce

romp to bounce around playfully like children or lambs in a field. But the word, usually as a noun, is a favourite of tabloid journalists. So, if you read; *football manager in Biarritz hotel romp* – then you'll know that a football manager has been caught out having it away in a hotel in Biarritz

romp in the hay a sexual experience

rose → **a rose by any other name** TRUNCID *a rose by any other name would smell as sweet*; from Shakespeare's Romeo and Juliet, the phrase is used to mean that what something or someone actually IS is more important than what it or they are called

Rosie Lee [RHYMING SLANG] tea; *what the English drink a lot of, you know, Rosie Lee, you and me, tea!*

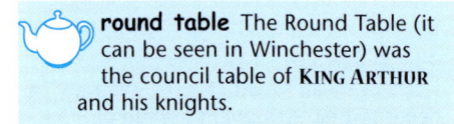

> **round table** The Round Table (it can be seen in Winchester) was the council table of **KING ARTHUR** and his knights.

Royal Scot, the a famous steam engine (doesn't run any more)

Royal Society, the an old and venerable society of eminent scientists

royal we

> An individual member of the royal family is traditionally supposed to refer to his or her self in the plural. The usage descends to commoners:
> *I am up here trying to work and we would appreciate it if you lot down there could keep the decibel level down.*

rozzer [SLANG] a policeman

RP

> received pronunciation; what is regarded as the standard English accent, though its social importance is not quite what it used to be:
> *the requirement for news readers to be RP has long since disappeared*

RSPCA, the Royal Society for the Prevention of Cruelty to Animals; *their neighbours called the RSPCA because of the state the dog was in*

Rudolph (the red-nosed reindeer) the reindeer who, because of his shiny red nose, is just what Father Christmas needs to help him pull his sleigh of presents through the foggy winter nights

🦻 **Ruislip** [pronounced rye-slip]

> **Rule Britannia** a patriotic song, harking back to the days when the British navy ruled the waves. The famous chorus goes:
>
> Rule Britannia!
> Britannia rule the waves.
> Britons never never never shall be slaves.

S

SAE stamped addressed envelope

sainted → **my sainted aunt!** DATED COLLOQUIAL expresses surprise

Saints, the a nickname for the Southampton football team

🦻 **Salisbury** [pronounced solz-bree]

saloon bar like the PUBLIC BAR

Salop Shropshire

samosa a very popular Indian snack consisting of a triangular pastry case filled with spiced vegetables or meat

Sandhurst a college where army officers are trained, a seal of good quality; *new chap coming out next week, Sandhurst fellow*

Sandringham one of the royal family's homes; in Norfolk

SAS Special Air Service, the British army's élite section, trained especially in undercover and behind the lines operations

satnav a satellite navigation system used in cars, a map substitute

sausage dog COLLOQUIAL a dachshund

Savile Row a street where expensive (and traditional) tailors operate; *the Editor was very Savile Row, the PM by contrast rather Marks and Sparks*

scepter'd → **"this scepter'd isle"** Britain (from Shakespeare's Richard II)

school run MODPHEN not athletics or anything sporty, the school run is the daily drive by mum or dad to take the kid(s) to school, a road-clogging modern phenomenon

Scotland Yard 1) the headquarters of the London police force; 2) a shorthand for the London police force itself; *Scotland Yard are still looking into it*

Scouser COLLOQUIAL a person from Liverpool (also, more officially, called a Liverpudlian)

scratch → **I'll scratch yours** TRUNCID I'll help you out, if you help me; a truncation of *if you scratch my back, I'll scratch yours*

Scrooge a very mean person who is extremely unwilling to spend money, a character in Dickens' Oliver Twist; *go on, buy your kids an ice cream, you miserable old Scrooge!*

Scrubs, the short for Wormwood Scrubs, a prison in London

🍸 **scrumpy** very potent, rough, dry cider from the west of England

seam bowler a bowler who uses the seam of the ball to make it change direction

secondary school the next stage after primary school, taking students between the ages of 11 and 18

semi a semi-detached house, one building designed and built as two homes, one a mirror image of the other; *they grew up in an ordinary semi in Penge*

set book a book that has to be read and studied for an examination

7/7 The date of the London terrorist bombings on 7 July 2005 has been named 7/7 (following the pattern set in the USA by 9/11).

seven-year itch COLLOQUIAL what supposedly happens to a married man after seven years of marriage: an urge for new sexual experiences

Sherlock Holmes one of a bizarre breed of amateur gentleman detectives, whose acute intelligence and inspirational problem-solving skills would be brought to the rescue of the baffled police. He and his somewhat more plodding companion, Dr Watson, were creations of the writer Sir Arthur Conan Doyle; *trust you to figure that one out, bit of a Sherlock Holmes, eh?*

Sherwood Forest a forest near Nottingham where ROBIN HOOD supposedly lived

shilling long since defunct as a unit of currency (there were 20 shillings in a pound until 1971), the word lives on in some expressions: *not quite the full shilling, young Keith – he's not quite all there, that Keith*

short back and sides a man's haircut, very short above the ears and at the back, seen as the standard no-nonsense army haircut; the expression has lost some of its impact since skinheads knocked the long-haired layabout look for six

short-arse COLLOQUIAL a not very nice term for a short person

short leg go to CRICKET

shout → **it's your shout** COLLOQUIAL it's your turn to buy the drinks

Shylock from Shakespeare's Merchant of Venice, a character who wants his money, or whatever is due to him, at all costs, a person with no mercy or human kindness

sick building syndrome MODPHEN it's not that the building is in a bad way but that the people who work in it suffer from the constantly re-circulated air, non-opening windows etc

signal → "I see no signal" attributed to Lord Nelson just before the battle of Copenhagen. The admiral of the fleet, Parker, hoisted a signal telling Nelson to disengage. When told of this, Nelson put his telescope to his blind eye and said *I see no signal*. He then went on to win the battle.

silly mid-off go to CRICKET

silly mid-on go to CRICKET

silly point go to CRICKET

silly season a journalistic way of referring to the summer period, when Parliament is in recess and the papers are often hard-pressed for political news. So, stories which would not otherwise be considered news get printed; *that story about toads was a typical silly season feature*

sin → for my sins IDIOM When the English really want to say *I am pleased and proud to be...* they find it easier to say *I am... for my sins* – as though it were a punishment; *I'm now a professor, for my sins*

Sinbad single income, no boyfriend and desperate

Sir a title used before the first name of a knight or baronet, the lowliest rung of the aristocracy; *Sir Richard Rogers*

sir a polite way of addressing a man, especially a customer or someone in a position of authority; not used between equals in modern English; *can I help you, sir?*

Sir Humphrey a character in YES MINISTER whose name has become a synonym for an ingenious and articulate civil servant determined to get his own way and retain the status quo in spite of the wishes of his masters, the politicians; *his plans for departmental change came up against a small platoon of Sir Humphreys*

six feet under IDIOM dead and buried

skater COLLOQUIAL a young person who skateboards as a hobby and generally wears the clothes associated with this hobby

slap and tickle DATED COLLOQUIAL a canoodle, a kiss and a cuddle; *Graham and Joyce were having a bit of a slap and tickle in the kitchen*

slaphead COLOQUIAL a bald-headed man

slash → **to have a slash** SLANG to urinate; a rougher expression; women wouldn't use it

sleeping policeman COLLOQUIAL a speed bump on the road

slips go to CRICKET

Sloane (Ranger) COLLOQUIAL named after a select area round Sloane Square in Knightsbridge, a stereotypical upper-class person, especially a woman, who dresses in expensive informal clothes; *in the early days of her engagement Lady Di was still very much a Sloane Ranger*

sloaney SLANG the adjective to describe **SLOANE RANGER**-style things; *Prince William and his sloaney chums*

🎧 **Slough** [pronounced slao (to rhyme with Mao)]

smacker SLANG 1) pound; *50 smackers and it's yours*; 2) a big kiss

smackeroonee SLANG pound, has an obvious humorous tone

smallest room, the the toilet

Smith, John the clichéd way of hiding identity, because it is a very ordinary name

> policeman: *right son, what's your dad's name?*
> chav: *John Smith*
> policeman: *being funny, are we?*

Smith → W H Smith's® the major chain of English newsagents and stationers a branch of which is to be found in most towns of any size; also a bookseller

Smithfield (Market) the main London meat market, in the City of London, which has been on this same site for centuries

Smoke, the SLANG London

🍸 **snakebite** a drink of equal amounts of cider and lager

🍸 **snug** a small, cosy bar in some pubs where there is room for everyone to sit in comfort – as a non-regular you might feel out of place

So'ton Southampton

soapbox If someone gets up on their soapbox this means that he or she makes a strongly felt speech.

sob sob COLLOQUIAL comic strip language, expresses sadness or regret, often mockingly; *so you got ripped off, sob sob!*

sod-all SLANG 1) nothing; none; 2) no; go to ALL

soh sense of humour, as sought or offered in the personal columns

Soho an area in central London famous for its bohemian and literary image and its connections with the sex and entertainment industries

Somerset House an impressive neo-classical mansion on the north bank of the Thames; it was the place where all births, marriages and deaths were registered for England and Wales and, although the building is no longer used for this purpose, its name retains the association

Sotheby's famous auction rooms

Sotonian 1) from Southampton; 2) a person from Southampton

South Bank the area in London on the southern side of the river Thames, particularly the area between Waterloo and Blackfriar's bridges, where major cultural institutions, such as TATE MODERN, are sited

South Downs the Downs are really ups, since the name refers to the gently rolling, treeless hills on chalkland in some of the southern counties, especially Sussex; *he used to walk ten miles every day over the Downs*

SPLIT INFINITIVE 157

South Ken short for South Kensington, a fashionable area of London

Southwark [pronounced suthuck]

Speakers' Corner At the corner of Hyde Park, by Marble Arch, there is a place where any person can get up on their SOAPBOX and make a speech to anyone who cares to stop and listen. Speakers range from known politicians to nutters.

special a name brewers give to certain varieties of their beer which tend to be stronger or more intensely flavoured than their ordinary beers

Special Branch the branch of the police force that deals with crime that has a political side to it

speech day Usually at the end of a school year, this is the ceremony when prizes are given to the best pupils (and a few speeches are made).

spiffing DATED COLLOQUIAL very good; *spiffing party, old bean!*

splash the boots SLANG to have a pee; a jokey expression

split infinitive

> inserting an adverb between *to* and its *verb*. It is a widespread language myth that it is a mistake to do this:

> *to boldly go where no man has gone before*

spoonerism

> a mistake in speaking when the first letters or sounds of one word are swapped for those of another word in the same sentence, often with comical results:
>
> *you have tasted a whole worm*
> =
> *you have wasted a whole term*
> *why don't you drop by for a stink?*
> =
> *why don't you stop by for a drink?*
>
> A few expressions have achieved permanent status as honorary spoonerisms: *a pheasant plucker*

🍽 **spotted dick** a traditional steamed or boiled suet pudding stuffed with dried fruit, which gives it a spotted appearance

Spurs a nickname for Tottenham Hotspurs (London-based football team); the name is never used with *the*.

square leg go to CRICKET

Square Mile, the the CITY OF LONDON

squire as a form of address, typically from working-class male to another male of a higher class; *where to, squire?, the taxi-driver asked*

Staffs Staffordshire

Stamford Bridge 1) Chelsea's football ground; 2) a battle won in 1066 by Harold, the last Anglo-Saxon king of England, before his weakened army succumbed two weeks later to the invading Normans at the Battle of Hastings

stand-up COLLOQUIAL There have always been solo artists who perform as comedians. The stand-up or stand-up comedian has now become a genre. There are clubs where amateur, would-be stand-ups can get up on a stage and try to make a crowd laugh.

Stanley knife® a short, replaceable blade contained in a thick handle and used for various practical tasks

start → "I've started so I'll finish" I intend to finish (saying/doing) what I have started; from a TV quiz programme called Mastermind, in which the question-master (the late Magnus Magnusson) reminded participants that, if he had started reading out a question when the final buzzer went, they were still allowed to answer that question and score a point for the answer

Steptoe a much-loved sitcom from the seventies and eighties featuring the comical relationship between an old man, Steptoe, and the son he depended on, both RAG AND BONE men

St George Saint George is the patron saint of England. His flag: a red cross on a white background.

stiff upper lip Keeping a stiff upper lip means not showing emotion and, in particular, not showing annoyance or sadness when things go wrong. It is thought to be a traditional English characteristic and does still exist to some extent.

Stilton® the best-known English blue cheese, produced in Leicestershire, Nottinghamshire and Derbyshire, often eaten at Christmas. It is one of the few traditional English foods which are now protected by a trademark.

stockbroker belt a suburban area of expensive houses, especially in the HOME COUNTIES, such as would be inhabited by City workers and the like

stone me! SLANG expresses surprise or disgust

stone the crows! SLANG expresses surprise or disgust; *I can't afford that! stone the crows, I only make £80 a week!*

Stonehenge a ritual circle of enormous standing stones, sited in Wiltshire and dating from around 2500 BC. It's probably the most famous monument in England.

stout a strong, dark-coloured beer which is brewed with roasted malt or barley. Guinness is a type of stout.

Strolling Bones, the COLLOQUIAL a fond name for the not-so-very-young Rolling Stones

Sun®, the a tabloid newspaper, with some news, a lot of gossip and some big boobs

Sunday short for *Sunday newspaper*; *which Sunday do you read?*; *most of the Sundays carried the story*

🍽 **Sunday dinner/lunch** the English meal par excellence, the main course of which is a roasted joint of meat, served with gravy, potatoes, and a wealth of other hearty vegetables

Sunday Sport®, the a newspaper, but don't buy it for sports write-ups: it's all sex and scandal

🍽 **Sunday roast** a national institution; *the kids still come round once a week for the Sunday roast*

🍽 **supper** supper is generally a light evening meal and can be one of two things: either a snack, eaten quite late and after dinner; or just another way of talking about what most people refer to as dinner

Sven Sven has now gone. He was the manager of the England football team, a taciturn Swede.

Sweeney, the SLANG the FLYING SQUAD

sweet FA SLANG sweet Fanny Adams, meaning *nothing*; *and how much did I get in return?, sweet FA, that's what I got, sweet FA*

> **swinging sixties** the way this decade is thought of in England, when there was a huge liberalization of social and sexual styles and attitudes and much classic English pop music was produced

T

ta COLLOQUIAL thanks (but don't say it twice because that will mean goodbye)

ta ta COLLOQUIAL goodbye

ta-ta → **to go ta-tas** COLLOQUIAL to go for a walk, in baby talk

tabloids The tabloids are the newspapers that are perceived as less serious, less analytical, more sensationalist. Some of the quality press have now adopted a smaller tabloid format.

Taffie COLLOQUIAL a Welshman (or woman), humorous (or insulting)

take → **it takes one to know one** IDIOM used to belittle someone when they have made a disparaging comment of some sort, to imply that the speaker might have the same characteristics as the person being talked about;

> A: he's a right old lecher
> B: takes one to know one

take → **you can't take it with you** IDIOM enjoy life while you can

Tate, the Britain's major art gallery, its London galleries are Tate Britain, containing British works from the 16th century to today and the TATE MODERN

Tate Modern the foremost modern art museum in London, housed in a converted power station on the SOUTH BANK

taxpayers' money IDIOM money that has come out of the ordinary person's pocket; the term is used as a reminder that, when the government spends money, it tends to be money that has been collected from Jo Public; *look at the super-luxurious offices they put up for themselves – and it's all tax payer's money, you know*

tea The Brits drink vast quantities of tea. Tea is standardly taken with milk and, if you like, sugar; less frequently black and less frequently still with lemon. Tea comes in cups, not glasses, and can also be brewed in pots. Although there exists no formalized tea ceremony as such, drinking tea is the focal point for a chat or a heart-to-heart. And *a nice cup of tea* is offered as the cure for minor ailments and shock.

tealeaf RHYMING SLANG thief

tears → **in tears** a clichéd pun of traditional wedding ceremony speeches; *this is such a moving ceremony that even the cake is in tears (read 'tiers')*

teatime traditionally around 4 o'clock in the afternoon; *I'll pop round to give you the tickets around teatime* – a dying concept, a disappearing fixed point in the day

techie COLLOQUIAL a technically minded person, someone who looks after the technical side of things, especially in IT; *sorry, I can't handle enquiries about compression ratios, you'll need to talk to one of the techies*

technicolour yawn SLANG a vomit; *looks like someone did a technicolour yawn right outside the restaurant*

telegram → **you'll be getting your telegram soon, won't you gramps** The Queen doesn't actually send telegrams any more, but citizens do still receive a card from the monarch when they reach their 100th birthday. The idiom has stuck.

Telegraph®, the (short for the Daily Telegraph) one of the main broadsheet newspapers with a conservative editorial outlook

> **television licence** In Britian you need to pay for a licence in order to watch TV. The money collected partly funds the BBC. A number of specially equipped vans patrol the land, tracking down viewers who have not bought a licence.

> **1066** This is a date which every Brit will know. It's the year when William the Conqueror invaded England and defeated and killed King Harold at the Battle of Hastings, actually fought at a place now called Battle, in Sussex.

tennis → **anyone for tennis?** DATED a catchphrase with overtones of carefree, sporty (and possibly slightly silly) youth

terrace In Britain a terrace is a row of houses each joined to the other on both sides.

TES, the [pronounced tee-ee-ess] The Times Educational Supplement®, a weekly publication for the teaching profession

terrace

Tesco® the biggest of the UK supermarket chains; it is said that out of every £7 spent in British shops £1 is spent in Tesco's. With the chain rampantly swelling to spawn new stores in areas already sufficiently Tesco'd, many of the natives object to living in Tescoland.

test an international cricket or rugby match, usually one of a series

test match an international cricket match

TGIF thank God it's Friday

🔊 **Thames** [pronounced temz]

Thames Valley the area bordering the Thames to the west of London, especially Oxfordshire, Berkshire and Buckinghamshire, more of a dish than a valley

them

> is used as an equivalent for *those*; it's colloquial and strictly incorrect but not in the downmarket way that, say, *what* in *the people what I know* is; ***it's been one of them days***

> **them and us** expresses the idea of two different groups who are mutually hostile to or do not understand one another; ***we have to get over this old-fashioned them and us attitude***

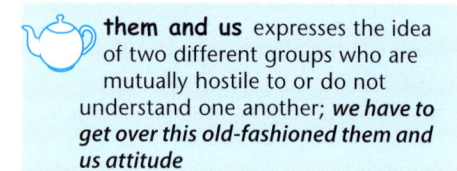

🔊 **Theydon Bois** [pronounced thayden-boyce]

third man go to CRICKET

thought → **it's the thought that counts** IDIOM it doesn't have to be an expensive present, as long as you do give a present; ***it's the wrong size and the wrong colour, but never mind, it's the thought that counts***

thousand and one an enormous number; *there are still a thousand and one things to be done*

throneroom SLANG the toilet, specifically the part where you sit down

ticketty-boo DATED COLLOQUIAL just fine; *now Linda and Ian are back together again and everything is just ticketty-boo*

Times®, the the oldest established national daily newspaper still in circulation, and one of the best-selling, it is a byword for good journalism

Times Lit Sup®, the The Times Literary Supplement

tin lid RHYMING SLANG a disparaging term: yid, Jew

tinkle COLLOQUIAL a phonecall, a ring; *I'll give you a tinkle tonight*

tiny feet IDIOM a reference to the birth of children, stereotypically made by new mothers-in-law and the like; *and when will we be hearing the patter of tiny feet then?*

Tipp-Ex® a white-out fluid

titfer RHYMING SLANG DATED (from tit for tat) hat

TLC tender loving care; *what these begonias need is a little TLC and they'll be as right as rain again*

TLS, the the Times Literary Supplement

toad in the hole a traditional and now rarely found dish of sausages baked in batter

toff COLLOQUIAL a posh person, well-spoken, well-dressed

tongue twister Why not test your English speaking skills with a couple of traditional tongue twisters?

> red lorries yellow lorries
> red lorries yellow lorries
> etc etc
>
> she sells seashells sitting on the sea shore
> does she sell seashells sitting on the sea shore?
> yes, she sells seashells sitting on the seashore

tootsie babytalk for foot

top → **on top** upstairs, if you're on a bus.

top hole DATED COLLOQUIAL usually as an interjection expressing great approval and pleasure; *still one bottle left? oh, top hole!*

topping DATED COLLOQUIAL very good, absolutely first rate

tosser COLLOQUIAL a robust insult for someone you think is being stupid, unhelpful etc; *sod off you dirty old tosser*

tosspot COLLOQUIAL a slightly milder form of tosser; *some media tosspot wanted to do interviews in the pub*

totty SLANG girls, women as seen from the point of view of the male out looking for some; *amazing totty at that club*

Tower, the the Tower of London

toy boy COLLOQUIAL the very young male companion of an older woman

trad traditional jazz

Trade Descriptions a reference to the Trade Descriptions Act, which is intended to control the quality of products and services relative to the way they are described and advertised; *no way is that Devonshire fudge, they could be in trouble with Trade Descriptions for that*

treble top A *treble top* is a darts term for the maximum score of 180

trick cyclist RHYMING SLANG psychiatrist

Trooping the Colour an annual ceremony of great pageantry on the date of the monarch's official birthday at which the guards regiments parade their regimental colours in the sovereign's presence

trouble and strife RHYMING SLANG wife; *a little argument with the trouble and strife, is it?*

Troubles, the the troubled relationship between Ireland and England

trousers → all mouth and (no) trousers IDIOM COLLOQUIAL a colloquial put-down, suggesting that someone, generally a man, brags but doesn't turn words into action; *poor Jim, she dumped him when she realized he's all mouth and trousers*

true-blue a true-blue Conservative is Conservative through and through

T-shirt → got the T-shirt TRUNCID the full form is *been there, done that, got the T-shirt*, the implication: that's nothing new to me; *Ibiza nightlife? yeah, got the T-shirt*

tube Americans might think that, if you see someone on the tube, you see them on TV. Not in Britian, though, where the tube is London's underground.

TUC the Trades Union Congress, the association of all trade unions in Britain

Tudor a 16th century style of architecture using a lot of brick and half-timbering, much imitated in the 20th century and often derided as suburban

tug-of-love used to describe a person caught up in the to-and-fro of a divorce case or relationship breakdown when a child is involved; *tug-of-love dad loses right to bring up toddler*

Turner Prize What the Booker Prize is to fiction, the annual Turner Prize is to visual art, and its sponsor, Channel Four, televises the awards ceremony, which adds to the buzz created by the prize. Much of the work presented has outraged the average person ('I could do better than that myself'), but it has also stimulated unprecedented public interest in modern art, and the four annual nominees have included many of British contemporary art's stars.

Turpin, Dick notorious as a highwayman in the early 18th century

TV Times a long-established TV listings magazine considered more downmarket than the Radio Times, of which it is the tabloid equivalent

Tweedledum and Tweedledee said of two people who are virtually indistinguishable, especially if they are always together. They passed into the popular imagination from Lewis Carroll's

Through the Looking Glass; ***voting is a waste of time, it's a choice between Tweedledum and Tweedledee***

Twickenham the main ground for international English rugby matches

Twickers DATED a slightly dated name for TWICKENHAM

two-one an upper second class degree

two-two a lower second class degree

U

UCAS [pronounced you-kass] the Universities and Colleges Admissions Service is the body to which people apply when they want to go to a university (used to be known as UCCA)

UHT milk milk that will last a long time because of the way it has been treated

UMIST [pronounced you-missed] the University of Manchester Institute of Science and Technology

Uriah Heep a character who oozes obsequiousness and whose huge desire to please makes him very unpleasant, from Charles Dickens' David Copperfield

us

> In colloquial language *us* can often mean *me*:
>
> *give us a look;*
> *help us with this bag, will you?*

V

V&A, the the Victoria and Albert (Museum) in London

Varsity Match, the an annual rugby match between the universities of Oxford and Cambridge, played at TWICKENHAM

Vatican roulette COLLOQUIAL having sex without contraception only at those times of the month when pregnancy is thought unlikely to ensue

Vera Lynn RHYMING SLANG gin (Vera Lynn was a famous and much-loved singer during WWII)

vgsoh very good sense of humour, as seen in the personal columns

vicar → **more tea, vicar?** IDIOM a remark jokingly made to fill an embarrassing silence in a conversation

Victor Meldrew a cantankerous (but somehow lovable) old man, from a popular TV series called One Foot in the Grave

VILLAGE GREEN

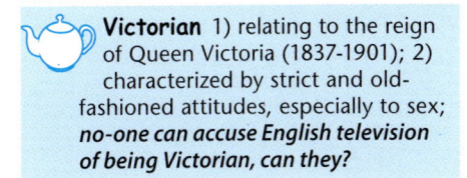

Victorian 1) relating to the reign of Queen Victoria (1837-1901); 2) characterized by strict and old-fashioned attitudes, especially to sex; *no-one can accuse English television of being Victorian, can they?*

Villa Aston Villa (football team from Birmingham); the name is never used with *the*.

village green A village green looms large in the image of the ideal English village. It's a plot of open, grassy land in the middle of the village which is used for communal activities and sports, preferably cricket. If it has a pond, so much the better; *let's go to that pub on the village green*

> **V-sign** No body language is more English than this; it can mean two things. Raising your hand to about chest height with the middle and index fingers in a V shape, if you make the gesture with the palm of the hand facing outwards it means 'V for Victory'. If you make the same gesture with the palm facing towards you, it means *fuck off*.

W

Wags wives and girlfriends (of the England football team)

wallop SLANG beer; though you can't say *a wallop*; ***fancy a pint of wallop?***; probably fading away now as a term

wally SLANG 1) a twit; 2) a gherkin

Walter Mitty 1) a person who has a fantasy life which contrasts strongly with his actual life; 2) a person who leads a double life; ***the church hall janitor turned out to be a Walter Mitty character who ran a drugs ring in Wapping***

wanker COLLOQUIAL 1) an insulting word for someone you strongly dislike for whatever reason, often because they are a bit pretentious; ***all the students think that***

WEATHER 179

lecturer's a bit of a wanker; 2) a person addicted to masturbation

War., Warks Warwickshire

🔊 **Warwick** [pronounced worrick]

watcher! COLLOQUIAL hello

Waterloo Station → **it's like Waterloo Station** IDIOM very busy and no privacy

Watford Gap the point about 70 miles northwest of London at which southerners supposedly think that the North begins and refined civilization as they know it ends; northerners, conversely, think that this is the point at which normal humanity peters out. It is the location of a well-known service station on the M1. Not to be confused with the larger town of Watford, further south.

Watson go to ELEMENTARY

we

> Doctors and nurses tend to use *we* as a replacement for *you* when talking to patients:
> *and how are we feeling this morning, Mrs Jarvis?*

weather so much of a national institution that it is often called just *the weather* rather than *the weather forecast*; *I watched the weather then went to bed*

wedding tackle SLANG a man's genitals; *some members of the squad might not have a problem with the paparazzi getting a shot of their wedding tackle*

well → **"didn't he do well!"** a catch line made famous by Bruce Forsyth in a TV quiz show, now used to express admiration but with a mocking overtone – and a silly voice – (the speaker for some reason not being able to utter: he did brilliantly!)

Welsh rarebit melted, seasoned cheese on toast, sometimes also written as *Welsh rabbit*

Wembley London's major sports arena, the home of football internationals

Wessex Although you'll come across Wessex in proper names, as a region Wessex no longer exists

West Country, the made up of Somerset, Devon, Cornwall, Dorset and parts of Wiltshire

West End, the a major shopping and entertainment area in London, to the west of the City of London

Western front → **all quiet on the Western front** IDIOM This simply means that all is quiet, that nothing much is going on, that there are no problems. The reference is to the film and novel of the same name about the horrors of WWI.

Westminster Westminster is the seat of parliament and is used to refer to it; *there has been discussion of little else at Westminster today*

whacko! DATED COLLOQUIAL an old-fashioned equivalent for *great, brilliant*, used as an interjection

what

> The use of *what* as a relative pronoun is common (and incorrect) in the south and southeast of England; *the flight what he caught got rerouted; the bloke what lives next to the pub*

what → **it's not what you've got (it's what you do with it)** IDIOM whatever money or talents you have, it's how you make use of them that really counts, not just possessing them

what-ho! DATED hello, can be used in mocking imitation of some supposed upperclass twit; *what-ho chaps, how about a couple of gins*

Which® a magazine that tests and reports on the quality of consumer products; *did you see what Which said about your new dishwasher?*

whistle RHYMING SLANG (short for *whistle and flute*) suit; *like the new whistle? pretty snazzy, eh?*

White City an area in west London famous for its stadium, now demolished, and for the BBC radio media centre based there

White Cliffs The White Cliffs of Dover, a kind of emblem for England and home; *so good to see those white cliffs again*

WHITEHALL 183

White Hart Lane the ground of Tottenham Hotspurs football team in London

White Paper a document outlining information or proposed government legislation on an issue

white van man COLLOQUIAL a mad driver, in a crazy hurry to get everywhere; will snarl you up in traffic; a menace on the roads

Whitehall Whitehall is where many government departments are situated; the name is used to refer either to the government (usually in a more administrative way) or to the civil service; *Whitehall has strenuously denied the allegations of delaying tactics*

Whittington, Dick a famous legendary figure, Dick Whittington rose from poverty to become Lord Mayor of London in the 15th century and his story is the archetypal poor-boy-makes-good tale. The Dick Whittington story is used as the basis of many **PANTOMIMES**. *Turn again, Whittington,* is a line most people know, meaning *go back and try again*.

> **Who's Who** an annual publication giving potted biographies of significant people in all areas of endeavour

> **WI, the** The Women's Institute, an organization devoted to the interests of housewives and women in general and which has considerable social and political clout

Wibbly Wobbly Bridge, the a nickname for the Millennium Bridge, which, when first opened to the crossing public, wobbled and vibrated to such an extent it was immediately closed for engineering adjustments

wide boy COLLOQUIAL Calling someone involved in any activity a wide boy means they are dishonest, unscrupulous and borderline criminal; *so then he comes along with his wide boy lawyer and threatens me*

Wilts Wiltshire

Wimbledon one of the world's major tennis events, associated with long, hot summers, strawberries and cream, and eternally frustrated English hopes of providing a winner

Winchester as well as being a town, this is one of the better known traditional English public schools, so if you hear someone say *he went to Winchester* they may well be talking education

Windsors, the the Royal Family

wltm would like to meet, in personal ads

Wolves a nickname for Wolverhampton Wanderers (football team); the name is never used with *the*.

Woolies COLLOQUIAL a nickname for Woolworths

Worcester [pronounced wooster]

🍽 **Worcester(shire) sauce** The English need sauces and spicy flavours in their food, and Worcester(shire) sauce meets both needs. First sold in 1836, this piquant brew generally contains soy sauce, vinegar, and spices, such as tamarind, can be added to many dishes and is an essential ingredient of a Bloody Mary.

Worcester woman COLLOQUIAL a type identified by pollsters, professional, white-collar, concerned about quality of life and likely to vote for whichever party promises to go for this

Worcs Worcestershire

world → **...est in the world**

> You'll often hear English (and British) people say that something English is the best in the world. This is a linguistic throwback to bygone days of empire glory. What people really mean is that something is very good, in their opinion. Clearly non-Brits are liable to find such utterances laughable or even insulting:
>
> *we will have a huge new casino and gaming palace in Manchester, but have no fear, we will also have the best gambling controls in the world*

Wormwood Scrubs a prison in London

worse for wear 1) worn out; 2) not in very good condition; 3) drunk

worse things happen at sea IDIOM a clichéd response to what is seen by some as a disaster, the implication being that there is always going to be someone somewhere who is having a tougher time, so don't worry and don't grumble; *value of your home dropped by half?, ah well, worse things happen at sea*

wotcha, wotcher SLANG hello, very southeast or Cockney

wrinklies SLANG old people

Y

Yard, the SCOTLAND YARD

Yardie a member of a criminal gang of West Indian ethnic origin

Yes Minister This is the name of TV series popular in the 1980s which followed the fortunes of a new and open-minded government Minister and his obstructive civil servant SIR HUMPHREY. Sir Humphrey clings at all costs to the status quo and is determined to thwart the Minister's plans; *according to the press the whole episode was totally Yes Minister*

Y-fronts® a traditional brand of male underpants with a panel opening framed in an upside-down Y, hence the name

yob culture MODPHEN a way of describing the kind of antisocial behaviour by young males (and females) that many people see as increasing in English society

Yorker a ball bowled in cricket in such a way as to hit the ground just under or just beyond the bat

Yorks Yorkshire

Yorkshire pudding not a sweet dish at all, but a traditional accompaniment to roast beef at **SUNDAY DINNER**. It is made of a light batter of flour, eggs and milk.

you and me RHYMING SLANG tea; *a nice cup of you and me*

yours truly COLLOQUIAL me, the speaker, a way of referring to oneself; *they all piled into the car and drove off but yours truly was left standing on the pavement*

Two maps of parts of England

*The **first map** shows the English counties. The Brits often have a strong emotional bond with their county of origin. They may be proud to be a Kentishman, have deep feelings for their Yorkshire roots or mysteriously profess to come from darkest Berkshire.*

Some counties to which the Brits still refer don't actually officially exist any more and aren't shown on this map. Cumberland and Westmorland are now merged into Cumbria. Huntingdonshire (or Hunts) is part of Cambridgeshire. And Middlesex, which you'll often read about in the papers, is mostly in Greater London.

*The **second map** shows the south and southeast, concentrating on larger towns and points of entry to and departure from the island. Most Brits live in these southeastern parts. In 2003 England as a whole had a population density of 383 people per square kilometre (compared with just 65 per square kilometre in Scotland). London had a population density of 4700 people per square kilometre.*

190 THE ENGLISH COUNTIES

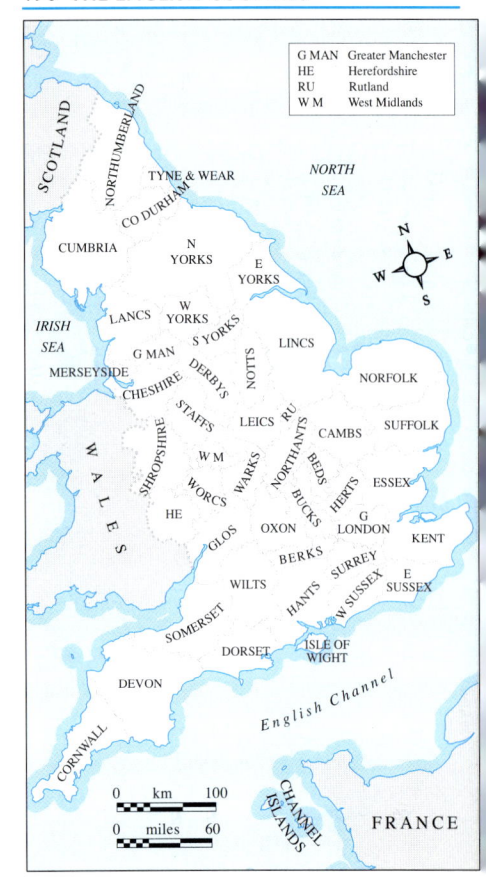

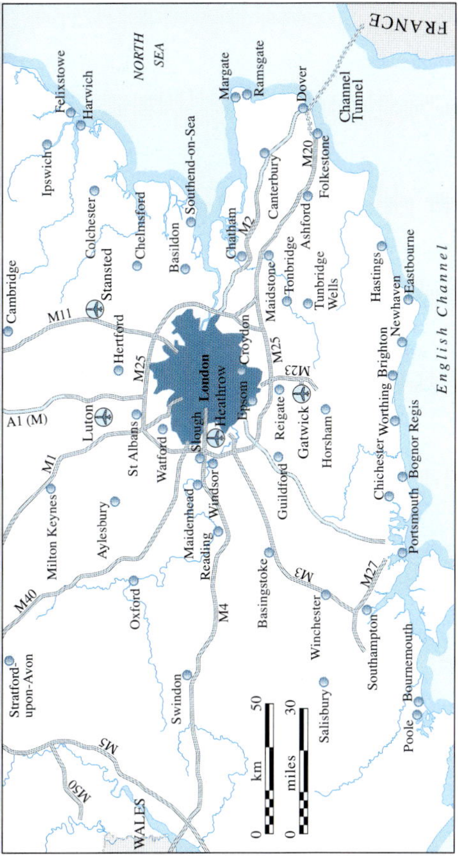

THE SOUTH AND SOUTH-EAST 191

also in this series

the Chinese Travelmate
the French Travelmate
the German Travelmate
the Greek Travelmate
the Italian Travelmate
the Japanese Travelmate
the Polish Travelmate
the Portuguese Travelmate
the Spanish Travelmate
the Turkish Travelmate

the Scots Travelmate
the American Travelmate

and more in preparation